Y0-BCI-000

Happy Birthday
1979

A Hundred Years of
SIAMESE
CATS

Also by May Eustace
CATS IN CLOVER
TOP CATS AND SOME OTHERS
FIFTY YEARS OF PEDIGREE CATS
(with Elizabeth Towe)
THE ROYAL CAT OF SIAM
THE WORLD OF SHOW CATS
MOSTLY ABOUT CATS

Copyright © May Eustace, 1978
First American Edition, 1978

Library of Congress Cataloging in Publication Data

Eustace, May.
    A hundred years of Siamese cats.

    1. Siamese cat — History.   I.   Title.
SF449.S5E85   1978   636.8'25   78-5007
ISBN 0-684-15783-7

Copyright under the Berne Convention

All rights reserved. No part of this book
may be reproduced in any form without the
permission of Charles Scribner's Sons.

1 3 5 7 9 11 13 15 17 19 I/C 20 18 16 14 12 10 8 6 4 2

Printed in Great Britain

Photograph: Dr. B. R. Eustace

Hawthorn Sunya
Seal Point kitten. Bred and owned by author.

A Hundred Years of SIAMESE CATS

by May Eustace

CHARLES SCRIBNER'S SONS
New York

For Lady Wilson
who has graciously accepted
the dedication of this book.

ACKNOWLEDGMENTS

I am indebted to the many cat owners and photographers in different parts of the world who have sent me photographs for inclusion in this book. My only regret is that it was not possible to use them all. I also wish to thank Mr. R. Renaut for his drawing of the cats' heads, included in the text. My grateful thanks are also extended to Lady Wilson for accepting the Dedication. All fanciers know of the appreciation and love given to the first Siamese to take up residence in 10 Downing Street.

I am always mindful of the friendship and kindness shown to me by the British Cat Fancy. Especially is remembered with affection Mrs. Elizabeth Towe, my collaborator in *Fifty Years of Pedigree Cats*.

To *American Farm and Home* thanks are due for allowing me to print little Cindy Hearne's attractive poem; also thanks to the Hon. Mrs. Michael Joseph for permission to publish poem — *To a Siamese Cat*.

A special word of thanks will not be out of place for my Editor, Barry Shaw, who ploughed so industriously through reams of cat appraisal and produced this book; and to my son, Brian, now resident in Canada, for his photography and interest in his mother and her cats.

Contents

1 Origin   7

2 Reflections of the First Fanciers   16

3 And the Years Rolled By   28

4 The Siamese Cat becomes a Show Cat   43

5 The Siamese becomes a Pet Cat   56

6 Breeding   65

7 Kittens and Their Care   75

8 Goodbye to all that   90

CATS

I like cats.
Fat cats, crawl into hats cats,
Small cats, play with ball cats, also tall cats,
Fun cats, sun cats,
Cats that have names, cats that play games,
Hot cats, fall into pot cats,
Laying cats, playing cats,
Good mood cats, good food cats,
Cats that eat mice, cats that are nice,
Cold cats, old cats, nice strong bold cats,
Cats with mittens, cats with kittens,
I like cats!

Cindy M. Hearne — aged nine

Courtesy of *American Farm and Home*,
Canadian Edition, Almanac 1975.

1. Origin

Thanks to the naturalists and historians who first kept records the arrival in the West of the Siamese cat is known to have been just one hundred years ago. Wherever he first showed his face the biographers noted him down as a pretty one. Then his association with humans made him prettier still. A hundred years of love, devotion and careful breeding has brought into our lives this perfect little being — unquestionably the greatest of all additions to the feline race. Reading our history books we find that aeons of time have passed since the first cat appeared on the earth. In fact very little is known about his origin and creation; there is however tangible proof of his first domestication. And again aeons and aeons of time have clouded their true identification. We called them cats, merely just cats. Small carnivorous quadrupeds that, it was surmised, descended from a vicious little creature which inherited the earth millions of years ago. This creature was described as a Miacus, and was probably of the weasel and stoat family. But this is mostly conjecture. Those of us who love cats would place them, if we could, in the higher strata of the animal kingdom.

Sir George Mivart, the nineteenth century writer of *The Cat — An Introduction to the Study of Backboned Animals*, a highly technical book, said that the cat's original ancestor was probably some long-lost beast of the Order Insectivora, of which the hedgehog is the existing representative, and he claimed for our cat the

proud position of the highest form of mammalian
development — higher as an animal than even man
himself.

Again we are theorizing. Now back to reality.

The ordinary household cat, much as we know him
today, was an honoured guest in the palaces of the
Egyptian Pharaohs, about 4,000 years ago. As he lived
in the highest stratum of Egyptian society, so he died.
His remains were richly embalmed and he has been
found interred with kings and princes. Mummified cats
have also been discovered in crypts and tombs. Ancient
engravings now in the Egyptian Gallery at the British
Museum, for instance, clearly outline the feline form.
Bronze and copper figures of cats, dating from the early
middle ages, still exist.

Traders from Persia probably first brought cats to
Europe, along with their baubles and trinkets; the
Romans introduced them to Britain, the early European
settlers to America. So, man and cat walked side by side
for many centuries. Statesmen, soldiers, princes, poets
and artists have delighted in cats, who have known how
to ingratiate themselves. In Mark Twain's words: 'A
house without a cat, and a well-fed, well-petted and
properly revered cat, may be a perfect house, perhaps,
but how can it prove its title?'

Because of his poise and dignity, the cat has been
included in many of the world's greatest paintings.
Dürer's 'Adam and Eve' portrays a cat creeping into the
Garden of Eden; Rembrandt chose a cat to figure in his
painting of the Virgin and Child. Renoir, too, liked
painting cats.

But until about one hundred years ago, cats were just
cats. Except for variations in colour, they were much the
same. To cat lovers, cats were either 'Persians' or short-
hair variations of the ordinary domestic cat, none of
which was individual enough to merit a different appel-

lation. Then, in the latter half of the nineteenth century, a changing world for humans brought a changing world for animals. As dog fanciers emerged, dedicated to evolving and perfecting breeds of dog, so cat lovers formed a club and the British Cat Fancy was created. The names of Charles Cruft for dogs and Harrison Weir for cats were soon to be emblazoned across the world. Harrison Weir, F.R.H.S., was the greatest fancier of the age. He was a prolific writer and perfect illustrator. All animals came within his ken. He wrote for *Illustrated London News*, *The Field*, and *The Graphic*.

Shows, run in an organised manner, were adopted by animal lovers to further the appreciation and well-being of cats and dogs and to discourage mongrelism through indiscriminate matings.

The birth of the cat show meant the birth of the pedigree cat. Harrison Weir, endowed with the pioneering spirit of Cruft, set the first seal on what was to develop into one of the greatest and most exciting hobbies of this generation — the breeding and exhibiting of pedigree cats. Cats had something. They were far superior to the other small furry and feathered creatures that would come into our vision. Only with dogs could they compete. A domesticated cat is a being that can enter into our own world. He is fastidiously clean and respects our way of life. Soon he can become as one of the family.

And about this time, suddenly, there arrived, it would almost seem from outer space—this superb little creature — the Siamese cat! What a beautiful vision to set before a cat lover!

Harrison Weir gave a most enthusiastic welcome to the new addition to his list. There were so many of his fellow fanciers that wished to be associated with the new arrivals that the great man may have been forgiven if he had not quite all his facts right. John Jennings, another

Victorian writer and judge, and contemporary of Harrison Weir, complimented himself on recognising the value of the Siamese cat when they first appeared at shows in Crystal Palace in 1876-77, and claimed that he was instrumental in having rescued them from the "Variety" class, and had them placed in classes of their own. Frances Simpson, then one of the greatest authorities on show cats, collected facts about Siamese from reliable sources. Miss Forester-Walker, an official of the Siamese Cat Club, gave us a date to remember —exactly one hundred years ago. Miss Simpson's book, *The Book of the Cat*, contained 376 pages of splendid reading about every known breed of cat, and also 350 photographs. It is a classic in cat books that has bever been equalled. She dedicated it to Harrison Weir, and his acknowledgement in letter form, part of which is quoted, is almost like an obituary on a headstone:

> Miss Frances Simpson has kindly dedicated her labour of love the fascinating *Book of The Cat* to me, and truly the honour is great. Words cannot convey my feelings, but of its fullness the heart speaketh — Thanks . . .
>
> Far more, I might, and perhaps am expected to add; but my life's work is well-nigh done. He who fights honourably the good fight sinks at last. Frances Simpson has rendered me her debtor, and others, beside myself, will tender her grateful thanks for her work in the cause of the cat and for the welfare of the fancy. Adieu!

So the friendship and co-operation between these two cat lovers was firmly established, though not for long. The great fancier and benefactor of the Siamese cat died three years later, aged 82. But he lived long enough to see the Siamese cat accepted, and the standards he had set became the yardstick for future generations of Siamese breeders.

Soon Siamese cats were coming in from all places. It would have been impossible to keep track of this cat stampede. However, though there are still some unbelievers, it is an incontrovertible fact that two mature Siamese arrived in England from Bangkok about 1880, through one Owen Gould of the diplomatic service — a present to his sister, Mrs. Veley. From then onwards the British fanciers never lost touch with the cats from Siam.

Since most of the newly recognised breeds got their names from their place of origin, it was logical even without proof to believe that Siamese came from Siam, and they have been closely pinpointed to Bangkok. That they had many extras, not associated with the common cat, is also an inescapable fact. They were different in type and bearing, and came under the heading of foreign type. To support the theory of the Siamese cat's variance with fellow felines we have written words of the fanciers of that age. Each singled out a different angle with which to view the stranger from the East.

Mrs. Vyvyan, one of the pioneer Siamese cat lovers chose to emphasise an olfactory condition:

> It was observed by strangers that there is a "pleasant wild animal odour" about these cats which is not apparent to us.

Then we have the writings of Mrs. Cran, who was described as an authority on Siamese cats. In one of the first published magazines of the century — *Cat Gossip* — she endeavoured to give the Siamese a veneer of the unusual:

> A distinctive mark, and not an accidental one, was found on highly-bred Siamese. The priests consider such cats to be specially sacred and a God once picked up one and left the shadow of his hands forever on its descendants. The marks suggested that someone with sooty hands had lifted a pale-coated cat, gripping its neck rather low, leaving the distinctive mark.

Mrs. Veley, a sister of Owen Gould, who had the first recognized imports, wrote amongst other things about coat colour:

The natives, who admired and kept these cats called them by a name meaning "cats the colour of ash wood" to distinguish them from the common cat.

Another of Mrs. Veley's comments was on the agility of Siamese:

One interesting thing about the first cats was that they always jumped the threshold of an open door; the sills of native doors being raised, they acquired this habit and it took long to eradicate it.

Harrison Weir, though never owning a Siamese, visited many friends who owned them, and he wrote about something he had observed for himself:

I have had several opportunities to observe Siamese, as they went about their business. I noticed in particular the intense liking of these cats for "the woods", not passing along the hedgerows like the ordinary cat, but quickly and quietly creeping from bush to bush, then away in the shaws; not that they displayed a wildness of nature, in being shy or distrustful, nor did they seem to care about getting wet like many cats do, though apparently they suffer much when it is cold and damp.

From all quarters came deliberations from important cat lovers about the idiosyncrasies of Siamese, or Siamese-related cats. Dr. H. L. Hammond of Connecticut, who had made a study of these foreign breeds, remarked on the depth of their slumbers:

They have spells of sleeping when nothing has power to disturb them, but when they are awake they are immediately bright and high-spirited.

These observations, though they might be overlooked in the ordinary cat, sounded like magic to the ears of the Siamese worshippers. All along the line the theme song about the Siamese was that he was no ordinary cat. Anything fresh was welcomed by the diarist, Frances Simpson.

Mrs. Chapman, a visitor from Ireland to one of the first shows, wrote in *Cat Gossip*:

My husband rarely makes any comments about my cats, but about our English import, Wally Pug, I heard him tell the Vicar's wife that he was capable of uttering the most awful sounds. "No cat Mieau — Wally's — rather like the wailing of a banshee — if you know what I mean. These ghostly beings follow certain Irish families, and are meant to acquaint its owners of death and desolation to come. My wife says 'Rubbish', but I say 'Beware'." She then continued to admonish him, "Why, the lovely creature is only trying to talk to you."

And for the past 100 years, Siamese have continued to "talk" and at the same time make love.

Mrs. E. Buckworth-Herne-Soames, a dedicated Long Hair breeder, and writer, wrote of what she considered an annoying trait in Siamese:

Personally I have never kept Siamese though I had a very handsome one given to me many years ago, but she had the unfortunate habit of suddenly running up my back on to my shoulders, which so startled me that I gave her away to a real Siamese lover.

Legends abound about the Siamese cat. His kinked tail was the receptacle for the rings of the Eastern Princess, his squint was accounted for by an equally feasible explanation and his blue eyes were another gift from the gods. No other creature had so far captured the imagination of animal lovers. They clung tenaciously to Harrison Weir's description of Siamese cats as royal cats. They felt that this was a delicious title, and all agreed that it would do much to boost his ego.

And so, the little feline aristocrat made his début in the cat world. He was accepted as a royal cat from Bangkok — a city of temples, monasteries, museums, palaces, colour, glamour and romance — a fitting birthplace for a prince amongst cats. Here, in that portion of the city where dwelled the monarch and his courtiers, Siamese cats were found in plenty. This was a city of eternal movement. When the blinding glare of the rising sun illuminated the temples, Buddhist monks could be seen emerging from their highly coloured shrines where they had been holding their vigil with the gods.

And of all the temples, the most striking is the Reclining Buddha, which consists of a whole set of pagodas, temples, courtyards, ponds, statues, and everything that appertains to Eastern culture, and makes a common traveller from Europe sit up and take notice. The focal point is the huge statue of the Buddha — about 160 ft. long and almost 50 ft. high. The sight of it nearly takes one's breath away. When asked about its significance, the Thai people explain that the statue symbolises the passing from earthly life to Buddhist beatitude, which means the extinction of individuality and absorption into the supreme spirit. Built with brick and mortar and covered all over with gold leaf, and the soles of the feet adorned with mother-of-pearl, the effect is startling. Other temples are the Emerald Temple and the Temple of Dawn, which are impressive and beautiful.

The Siamese cat, as we have grown to know and love him, has kept much of the grace and charm of his homeland. The Thai dancers seen in Bangkok can execute intricate movements, wriggling about and showing mastery over their bodies akin to the striking attitudes of the Siamese cat when he plays about, or even whistles for dinner.

But how did he get here? Wherefore his creation? That he came from Siam is hardly disputed but his many claims to royal blood and to a distinguished heritage are questioned by the modern writers and zoologists. But those of us who love Siamese cling to our beliefs, we appreciate that he is the most distinguished of all breeds of cats and, whatever his origin, he is no ordinary cat.

Theo. F. Megroz, writing in 1933 for E. Buckworth-Herne-Soame's book on cats, was carried away with enthusiasm, giving the best write-up to this little cat he had before or since. He admits to his research ending in failure, but his belief that an aura of mystery and romance surrounds the Siamese cat was constant:

> Let us then, leave their origin a mystery — a mystery of the Orient. Sufficient that we have in the midst of our incertitude what might even be the incarnation of a divinity.

And so the story goes. The real origin of the Siamese cat will always remain a mystery. Many serious and deep-thinking modern writers dismiss the legends and Megroz's in particular as an absurd dream of the past. Even well-known Siamese lovers like the late Sir Compton MacKenzie disagreed with many theories about the origin of the Siamese cat, and wrote in his introduction to Phyl Wade's book:

> I maintain that the Siamese cat is a selected and inbred variant of the Malay jungle cat. It is, in face a semi-albino, and it is very noticeable that the same kind of colouring has been produced by selection and inbreeding with the Jersey cows.

Many important zoologists through the years have decided that the Siamese cat is nothing more or less than a freak cat — an albino — a semi albino, and that the colour pattern that distinguishes the Siamese occurs from time to time in many animals. Born white, within a few weeks the Siamese kitten begins to show markings on its nose, ears, tail and legs.

But though the colour pattern may be attributed to many variations in nature, it is, because it is combined with foreign type, blue eyes, and the oriental look that the Siamese is different. His whole shape and physique is completely at variance with other cats. To see a Siamese stalk his prey is to see a jungle cat in action. There is no mistaking his origin.

2. Reflections of the First Fanciers

Distinctive markings, royal affinity, glamour and the like could not have immortalised the Siamese cat and given it its place in the cat world. It was because it was identified and accepted as an entity, to be included in the names and varieties of cats in the register of the newly inaugurated Cat Club, that it became an established breed. Harrison Weir, the father of the Cat Fancy, found the study of cats to be all-absorbing. He was very familiar with the older breeds and these were easily classified, but he was overwhelmed with joy and excitement when he heard of the arrival of the handsome oriental — the Royal Cat of Siam. This was a newcomer to the feline world, with tradition and lineage behind it. To the mind of the great naturalist and cat lover this new and beautiful cat must not be permitted to lose its identity.

Harrison Weir wrote, after seeing Lady Dorothy Neville's Seal Point:

> Among the beautiful varieties of the domestic cat brought into notice by the cat shows, none deserve more attention than "The Royal Cat of Siam". In form, colour, texture, and length, and rather shortness of coat, it is widely different from other short haired varieties; yet there is little difference in its mode of life.

He then proceeded to establish Siamese in his list of show cats.

John Jennings, a cat judge and a contemporary of Harrison Weir, writing about the same time described the Siamese cat as:

The Siamese, or Royal Cat of Siam, by which name it is also distinguished, from the fact that it is propagated and protected under Royal supervision, is without doubt a magnificent animal and well worthy of the kingly patronage. A pure-bred Siamese is a valuable cat, especially the male, for like the Chartreuse monks' productions, as previously described, the majority are rendered neuter. This, when we consider how the male influences outward characteristics, may, in a measure, explain why several what I call "off colours" are now and again exhibited as Siamese, a cross probably between a pure-bred Siamese female and our short hair self coloured male cat. The special colour of the Siamese is a clear dun, with no trace of sooty blemishes on the body. The extremities, viz. nose, ears, feet, and tail have black markings, and those on the nose should extend and encircle the eyes. The coat is particularly short and close in texture, even and brilliant and the eyes are deep blue in the pure breed, and are therefore important.

So Harrison Weir and John Jennings had similar thoughts about the Siamese cat.

Later in Frances Simpson's *Book of The Cat*, the stages of the development of the breed were well explained and illustrated. In her introductory notes to a large and well-written chapter she wrote:

I have often remarked at our cat shows that strangers in the Fancy will enquire and ask to be directed to the Siamese section, and many and varied are the exclamations of surprise and admiration expressed on seeing, perhaps for the first time a row of Siamese cats in their pens. Nor is it always necessary to direct visitors to the Siamese classes, for generally these animals will betray their whereabouts by the unique tone of their voice. There is certainly a great fascination about this peculiar breed of cats which is yearly becoming more popular and fashionable.

This was written prior to 1900, about thirty years after the Siamese cat's first known appearance in public. Even the greatest authorities, and Frances Simpson certainly was one of them, were impressed. All agreed that his coming was an event of great importance, and the early owners of Siamese cats treasured the idea of their exclusive association with Royal families of Siam. M.

Oldfield Howery, surveying the Siamese scene much later, introduced thoughts of the spiritual:

> Ancestor worship is still an impelling force in Oriental countries. It was probably in order to show reverence to the departed monarch that when the young King of Siam was crowned in 1926, a white cat was carried by the court chamberlains in the procession to the Throne Room. Even today the Burmese and Siamese believe that the beautiful sacred cats enshrine the spirits of the dead, so, when a member of the royal house of Siam was buried, one of his favourite cats used to be entombed with him.

Mivart, so often studied by those who want the truth about the early history of cats, wrote in 1881:

> The Royal Siamese is one of uniform colour, which may be of a very dark tinge. There is a tendency to a darker colour in the muzzle — as in pug dogs. It has also remarkable blue eyes, and sometimes, at least, two bald spots on the forehead.

In most of the early books on Siamese, we hear their body colour described as "dun". As some dictionaries explain that the colour "dun" as grey, dark and gloomy, we are happy that the colour "dun" is omitted from modern standards.

It was recorded by reporters at a Cyrstal Palace show about 1876 that there were some very odd looking cats on exhibition. These were described as having black muzzles, ears, feet and tail, and their coats were drab and "dun" in colour. Of course these were our first Siamese.

My writing may be too filled with quotes; nevertheless I cannot ignore the remarks of an old-time judge, H. C. Brooke:

> To the search for something new we owe the beautiful Siamese. But the eulogies of these first fanciers were soon changed to a different key. The new race of cats had not the stamina or the staying power of the little cats of an earlier age. New owners found themselves up against a stone wall. The Siamese cat was the most prolific of all breeds, and the mortality amongst young stock was alarming. As everyone with any pretence at being a fashionable fancier set about breeding Siamese, their welfare became everyone's concern.

Catteries which formerly housed Long Hairs now opened their doors to the Siamese. It was found that they were good mixers with other breeds, and this enhanced their popularity. Neither did their intelligence and friendly charm go unnoticed.

But soon, alas! the Siamese cat was a stricken cat. Disease in many tortuous ways attacked it from every angle. Losses were so great that there was a real threat to the existence of the breed. It is certain that the worst might have happened had not so many people of wealth been able to pay handsomely for replacement of the fast-diminishing stock. Worm infestation was so serious that it did not seem possible to control it. Whole catteries were affected, and, after it had spent its course, the few remaining weaklings were rendered useless for breeding. Then came feline enteritis, which pursued its victims relentlessly. There was no let-up for there were no known treatments. Kittens, too, that were seemingly healthy at birth, just faded out. This was heart-break time for the Siamese breeders and owners.

Miss Cochrane, a vice-president and founder member of the Siamese Cat Club, a judge and a very much respected fancier of the day, made public her regret at the short life enjoyed by so many Siamese cats:

> Alas! that these little companions to whom we are permitted to become so deeply attached should be only lent to us to brighten our weary way for so short a period. "To To" was always very delicate, and after lying at death's door on several occasions she finally entered in; with her last breath she crept into my arms to die.

Miss Armitage, another important fancier associated with the Siamese Club, sustained many losses through infection, which, she said, she had contracted at shows:

> My adored Sam Sly, returned with me from Manchester, festooned with honours and medals, but only arrived home in time to place his head on his pillow and die. Another of my prize cats, "Royal Siam", who came from the royal Palace, is

a splendid specimen, but I would not risk him at public stud.
I allow a few selected friends to bring their queens to him.
Neither have I ever shown him, for he is too precious a pet to
be allowed to run risks.

Show cats took the biggest tumble, and Siamese classes
at shows diminished rapidly and there were wholesale
cancellations. Few breeders would risk their valuable
cats in public. It was so bad that show promoters thought
it wiser to omit Siamese from their schedules.

Yet the Siamese hung on tenaciously to life and we
read of their American début. Mrs. Clinton Locke
welcomed English-bred Siamese to the U.S.A. in 1902.
After a trial period in which acclimatization was a careful
process the imported cat prospered and, during the first
decade of the century, there emerged from the show scene
a Siamese Champion called Madison California.

But soon all was not well. The Siamese began to lose
ground. The American publications *Our Cats* and *Cat
Review*, recorded that Americans were not breeding good,
healthy Siamese. They appealed to English breeders for
help. As far as they were able they responded immediately
and shows kept going, with or without Siamese patronage. There has always been a very strong tie between
fanciers the world over.

They say the first cat show held in America at Madison
Square Gardens in 1895 was organized by an Englishman,
James H. Hyde. He had been fired with enthusiasm by
attending a cat show at the Crystal Palace, London.
After that, as in the mother country, many cat clubs were
organized. The Beresford Cat Club was founded in 1889
under the presidency of Mrs. Clinton Locke. This set the
seal to the great days that were to follow. It was said that
many of the best people in the U.S.A. were members and
on the honorary list were such names as Lady Marcus
Beresford, Louis Wain, Helen Wilmslow, Madame
Ronner and Agnes Repplier. All cat lovers at the end of

the century to the present day will have read and enjoyed the beautiful writings of Agnes Repplier. After the death of her adored cat Agrippina, her tributes run:

> Dear Little Ghost,
> Whose memory has never faded from my heart accept this book, dedicated to thee, and to all thy cherished race. Sleep sweetly in the fields of asphodel, and waken, as of old, to stretch thy languid length, and purr thy soft contentment to the skies. I only beg, as one before me begged of her dead darling, that, midst the joys of Elysium, I may not be wholly forgotten.
> Nor, though Persephone's own puss you be
> Let Orcus breed oblivion of me.

Glamour and glitter illuminated the early shows. The organizers had the right ideas. They knew they must draw in the public if they were to survive. It didn't seem worth while to put a cat into a plain pen, lying on straw, in drab surroundings, and shout, "Halt, Look to the right! This is a Siamese cat!" or, "Here is a Persian". No! Where was the appeal they asked each other? How could they attract the judges or the passerby?

Then Frances Simpson got to work, giving hints to exhibitors:

> Pink coloured ribbons are the most becoming to Blue kittens until their eyes have changed, then orange or yellow will be found more suitable. It is a mistake to tie very broad ribbons round your cat's neck when sending them to a show, I should choose a colour to match the eyes, with half an inch to three quarters in width. Tie a neat bow and give a stitch in the centre. Don't leave too long ends. Orange is the most becoming colour for Blue cats.

About pen decoration she had more to say:

> If you are allowed to provide pussies with cushions at a show, let the neck ribbon correspond in colour, as this will have a better effect.

About the tallies Miss Simpson advised:

> The metal tallies sent for the cats at show time will hang gracefully round the neck if a slip ring, such as is used for

fastening buttons, is run through the hole of the tally, and
then the ribbon is put through the ring. Let me advise narrow
ribbon, or if a broad bow is more stylish fold the ribbon half
the width round the neck and then tie. In this way pussie's
ruff will not be interferred with.

Miss Simpson took her cats very seriously and did not
tell many jokes about them, but the story of the little lady
cat which visited her stud is well worth re-telling over
and over again for it is doubtful if such an incident will
ever occur again. Very fashion conscious, and always
caring for the need for warmth at times, she advised cat
owners to make little jackets to wrap round a cat. It was
not surprising that a cat owner, having read Miss Simpson's show notes with particular emphasis on the
necessity for warmth, sent her little cat to Miss Simpson's
stud attired, as she herself described her:

> "A little lady was sent to my stud the other day clothed in a
> very smart jacket, through which her front paws were placed
> and it was buttoned up to the neck. This puss had also a pair of
> washleather boots on her back legs, so her appearance was a
> little startling!"

And in addition to the titivating of the exhibits, pioneer
show producers introduced many and varied classes.
There were special prizes for big cats, fat cats, small cats,
pretty cats, unusual cats, and there were classes named
after certain professional people, like doctor's cats,
lawyer's cats, poet's cats, writer's cats, and also the more
lowly were brought into the picture. The workman's
cat, the gardener's cat, the kitchen cat — all could win
separate prizes. This was fun and caused much friendly
rivalry. The best known of the workman's cats was in
Edinburgh, the cabman's cat. A well-known resident
lady was so impressed with a cabman's humanity in
rescuing a cat from imprisonment that she had a beautiful
shelter constructed and it was known as the Cabman's
Shelter, and existed for many years.

But the establishment of the Cat Fancy proper abolished many of these frivolities, and by the time the Siamese had entered the show scene he appeared in his own pen, hoping to win points by conforming to the required standards laid down by the Governing Council. Of course decorated pens can still be seen as side shows, and are very popular on the Continent and in America and Canada. But the cat in competition must appear unadorned, and as such is judged. This practice is universal.

Many changes in the manner of arrangements about the show cats took place. In the early decades of the century cats could be sent to shows without the owner or his representative being present. The organiser had a difficult task as the well-being of the cat was his responsibility. He had to pen and feed the cat and see to his general comfort during the few days he was away from home. The Blue Arrow train which was specially adapted for transport of animals was generally used. An officer of the club organising the show put the cat, properly secured and addressed clearly, on the train and it was safely delivered back to its home. *Cat Gossip* wrote that there were few cats lost in charge of the railway company.

And so, with many extra innovations, the new-look twentieth century cat show became established. Owners and breeders of class cats were given great incentives to keep breeding to high standards. Many valuable prizes could be won and shows were patronised by the greatest ladies in the land. Though far from being as robust as our British cats, the Siamese cat never quite lost touch with shows, though there were times when it seemed he would have to pull out permanently. Prone to respiratory diseases, his owners were very wary about exposing him to the draughts and exposure which could not be avoided at shows; yet he survived and in the early decades of the century he appeared in his own class at all-breeds shows, and numbers kept increasing. So many of these early shows have been written up by modern writers that repetition here is unnecessary. Old catalogues and old copies of *Fur and Feather* told their happy tales. As the keeping of records was not done with such meticulous care as it is done today, many important cats won their honours and disappeared. Also the practice of some breeders of calling their cats names like Tian the First, Tian the Second, Tian the Third, ad infinitum, caused confusion. Complicated though these pedigrees were, with many errors occurring through the system of numbering not naming, we did manage to get some of the facts right. The Siamese Cat Club sponsored by Major Woodiwiss, Hon. Secretary, created a Siamese register in 1924 and things improved. Testified records helped to dispel legend and to give succeeding generations of Siamese cat lovers a more accurate description of the first beginnings of registered Siamese cats.

The Great War (1914-1918) struck at the heart of the happy civilised life in Britain. Siamese cats were almost obliterated, as shows became quiescent and the nation's forces were concentrated on producing food and fighting for survival. By reason of our mundane needs we lost contact a little with our American fanciers, who, though they were under the strains of a bitter war too, managed to keep some of their hobbies going. Later it was known that they sent new stock to England. Over the years the American cat fancier and the British cat fancier sought no isolation from each other and a great and lasting friendship grew up between our two great cat fancies.

From the odd Siamese pet cat that survived on the crumbs that fell from the rich man's table in war-stricken Britain, a new race of Siamese quickly grew up. As soon as the war ended, hobbies were revived and cat shows once again were inaugurated. Though in many respects normality was slow to return, hobbies of special interest to women were almost immediately launched.

So quickly did the interest in Siamese cats revive that by 1924 there were sufficient Siamese cats in England for them to hold a show for Siamese only; in America, the same thing happened a few years later. Ours was held at the Pilbeach Gardens Hall, Kensington. Only two judges officiated. These were well-known women, Mrs. Cran and Miss Lea. Mrs. Cran was always interested in Siamese and I have recorded her impressions of the first Siamese. She was a very capable writer in many fields of animal activity. Miss Lea's name was associated with the National Cat Club, and also with the Orange, Cream, Fawn and Tortoishell Society. Altogether there were about ninety exhibits. The two Challenge Certificates were won by Miss C. Fisher, with her Seal Pointed Siamese. There were also Chocolate Pointed exhibits but these were not considered good enough to win the main awards.

It is interesting to observe that from 1920 onwards changes had hit the cat fancy, and at most shows men as judges were in the minority. We must remember here that "Votes for Women" were still not with us. How happy Helen Winslow would have been to witness the change. In her book written in 1900 she deplored the absence of women judges, in spite of the fact that the men were of very high calibre, including Harrison Weir, to whom she gave his full title F.R.H.S. and the well-known cat artist, Louis Wain. She wrote:

> In England there are seven judges, including two or three women; in America we should at least have one woman.
> A cat should be handled gently and kept as calm as possible during the judging. Women are naturally more gentle in their methods, and more tender-hearted. When my pets are entered in competition, may some wise, kind woman have the judging of them!

And so, with Helen Winslow's blessing, women almost swamped the judging arena. Their "tender hearts" won the day. It was mostly women who handed out the honours to our top Siamese; of course there were some men who attained fame as judges, but only a few. In recent years happily, it is thought, there are equal votes for men.

The British judge has always been a person much respected for his integrity and intelligence, and as such has been in demand for judging from all parts of the world. There are few countries with a council-controlled cat fancy, in which a British judge has not officiated and been made very welcome. Also standards for Siamese almost everywhere have been based on the first standards drawn up by the Siamese Cat Club. A British champion can hold his head high in any cat circles in the world.

The steward plays an important part in the running of a show. As he is probably aspiring to be a judge, he takes note of the judge's deliberations and notes the awards. A judge is usually happy to pass on his opinions of the exhibit placed before him. Inwardly he will take note of the bad points, which may not be noticeable on first sight. In the case of an adult, where Challenge Certificates are awarded a judge has to be very careful that the cat is a worthy winner. He studies his overall appearance, his type, his eye colour, and set, which must be oriental in the case of a Siamese; next his coat colour and texture, the length of his tail, and whether it is whipped or otherwise, his general condition, and then he assesses his value in comparison to others in the class.

The following is an extract from John Jennings' book *Age and Fecundity*, published in 1890:

> I have heard that cats have lived to the good old age of thirty years but the oldest that I can vouch for personally reached twenty-four years. The following scale of ages, on which the average period of a cat's existence is given as fifteen years, although somewhat of a digression, may interest those who delight in comparisons:
>
> An elephant lives 400 years

A whale, 306
A tortoise, 100
A camel, 40
A horse, 25
An ox, 25
A lion, 20
A bear, 20
A cat, 15
A dog, 14
A sheep, 10
A rabbit, 9
A squirrel, 8
A guinea-pig, 7

These extreme ages that are reached also point to fine constitutional development, careful housing and proper feeding. Dr. Stradling, who interested himself in *Curious Cats*, related that his cat followed him like a dog, and he had an extraordinary liking for potatoes, preferring even the raw peelings to meat. This cat lived to 18 years and the writer thought that his diet might have had something to do with his attaining this great age.

3. And the Years Rolled By

The twenties passed and all the time Siamese were establishing themselves. Champions were being made up regularly at shows which were held by the affiliated clubs. Agricultural show promoters were soon aware of the attractions pedigree cats had for the public. So, in conjunction with their own big shows in which every kind of livestock appeared, they held many Exemption cat shows. Exemption is the name given to the shows which had permission by the Governing Council to take place. Clubs can progress to Sanction and then Championship shows. The rules for the latter are very strict, and only well-established fanciers can be show managers. And as the clubs made progress, so did the Siamese. They were in on everything.

Cat exhibitions, apart from organised shows, proved to be very good publicity for Siamese. Here there were no rules, and pen decoration was encouraged. At the big agricultural and flower shows, marquees which housed cats were very popular. Most people had read about Siamese but had never seen them, and, when the cats were in playful mood, the spectators adored them.

Just as everything was going well, World War II put paid to our hobbies.

This war was a very personal war because it happened in the lifetime of many of the senior judges and fanciers. Any gathering of us could talk nostalgically of the good old pre-war days, which would never come again. Peace,

Yes! but never again the plenty of 1939! The war went on for so long that many of us can hardly remember the date of its ending. Though officially it was in 1945, the real ending did not come until much later, when rationing ceased and wartime restrictions were lifted.

During the war suffering was universal. We all suffered. Our children suffered. Our home-life suffered — especially when we were left without husband and father. Our animals suffered, but not with such devastating effects as those living in the Channel Islands; here there were mass exterminations, and many a heart broke as the owner took his beloved and loyal pet to the gas chambers. The Germans were coming and this was the edict issued to the people staying behind "Cut down on everything not required for human survival". The battle was on.

As in World War I all activities not concerned with the war effort were cancelled. Our hobbies and shows were the first to go. Again the Siamese cat was the first to fall by the wayside. To keep him alive he had to have special care about his food. To the little common house cat, we could say without recrimination:

> Come on now Daisy, there is a war on and there are mice down there in the valleys; also breadcrumbs are getting scarce and many little birds are just giving themselves up. Make haste my darling, but do come again.

And the little companion of our hearth managed to eke out an existence, and came back, none the worse for earning an honest, or dishonest living.

But in spite of everything a very small number of Siamese cats managed to survive, and this small nucleus emerged in 1945 to start a new race of Siamese. In the North of England where I lived during the war years, we were not so badly off as those living in the London area. Few bombs fell and as Blackpool was an evacuation centre we had some extra blessings. There were some surprises floating about and when my husband was demobbed he was able to procure for me a Siamese kitten. This little fellow was located through an advertisement in the paper. I never knew who his father was or his owner either. I do know he was not registered; like the evacuees, he was without any home or patronage.

But this is a sad tale to tell. I called him Jimmy, much to the annoyance of my husband, who always believed that Siamese cats had royal blood and must have a royal christening. However his name did not matter much as he did not live more than a month. His main diet, as stated by his breeder, should be cod's head, and there were plenty of these about. The fishmonger was kind and sent me such a pile of this kind of offal that its smell nearly took our breath away. And poor little Jimmy didn't think much of it either, for the only parts he found edible were the cod's eyes. He turned his back on us when we did not provide meals of cod's eyes only. He was desperately unhappy and we decided that he should have each of our portions of good fish in turn. Even this he would not have, and we were desperate. You could see him become a little shrunken shape and the little meat he had fell off his bones. The veterinary surgeon called, gave him an injection, and dismissed him as cured. Poor Jimmy! the little rich boy with the plebeian name, he just gasped and died. We immediately found the cause; worms, the killer of so many Siamese kittens. I looked up my cat books and read of the early days of Siamese when even the richest people in the land could not eradicate worms. Lady Dorothy Neville, a contemporary of Harrison Weir's, wrote to him about her Siamese cats in the last decades of the nineteenth century:

> I think these cats are exceedingly docile and domestic, but delicate in their constitution; although I kept one for two years, another over a year, but eventually all died of the same complaint, that of worms, which permeated every part of their bodies.

And so that was the story of my first Siamese kitten! He died of the complaint that had killed so many swanky kittens fifty years before.

Losing Jimmy so suddenly, and I would say, so tragically, was a great blow and I was determined when things were easier to look out for another Siamese. This did not happen until 1950, as I had busied myself in the meantime adding another human son to the family. Dominic was my last, and as soon as I had got him from under my feet I remembered Jimmy and went wholeheartedly into Siamese cat breeding, a hobby that has practically engulfed my life ever since. With my children almost out on their own, and my husband busily working on reducing his golf handicap I felt free — free to indulge myself, free to surround myself with the dearest little animal creatures nature could provide me with — free to do just what I liked with what I wanted.

In the North of England where I lived then we did not have any established cat club, or any clues as to where one could find pedigree stock and do things in a professional way. We found out that there was once a Northern Counties Cat Club, which had held shows in varying venues in Newcastle, Manchester and Leeds. But this club had disappeared in 1939, and left without trace. When the club was revived in 1957 the founders, myself included, made great attempts to locate anyone or anything to do with it. Everywhere we tried we met with negative responses. Lock, stock and barrel the old Northern Counties Cat Club had disappeared. We applied to the Governing Council to start again, and permission was granted, but before this permission was given to us there was a lot of shuffling and shilly-shallying. Certainly we got a cool reception. Mr. Hazeldine, the then chairman, intimated that they had more than they wanted, and where would they get a table large enough to seat any new delegates. However . . . they might consider a new Northern club, if . . .

Surprising as it might seem there were still quite a few Siamese about. Almost immediately on cessation of hostilities shows were again inaugurated. The Nottingham and Derby Cat Club was the first one to hold a show and, though there should have been a shout of jubilation for the heroes of Britain and the cats that they own, it was really a bad one for Siamese, as, once again the Siamese proved easy victims to disease and quite a lot just made their post-war début and died. All through the years many were born only to die. With Siamese it has always been a cry of the survival of the fittest.

Nevertheless shows soon became very numerous again, and the National Hall, Olympia, was the venue for many post war shows. Many events of national interest were celebrated by the holding of Championship shows. By the early sixties research on many feline diseases had proved successful and inoculations against feline enteritis and other contagious diseases were used and there was a better standard all round for show cats, especially for Siamese. Those, if inoculated when kittens, were better able to cope with emergency illnesses. At one time the Governing Council tried to introduce compulsory inoculations against enteritis, but failed. All cat breeders will agree that Feline Infective Enteritis, correctly named Panlenkopenia, is the Black Death of this age. An epidemic of F.I.E. in a cattery will leave a permanent scar on the heart of a cat lover.

The interest in Siamese grew so rapidly in Britain that many clubs especially for Siamese alone were founded. For foundation to be real they had to be accepted by the Governing Council. This was a way to give permanence to their hobby for the Governing Council, composed of delegates from the various clubs, presides over the destiny of the British Cat Fancy. At one time there was a preponderence of delegates from the Long Hair clubs but the popularity of the Siamese suddenly looked like

Photograph: Dr. B. R. Eustace

Siamese and Manx. From a painting. And below: An illustration taken from an ancient book, date unknown, with verse describing the cat. Courtesy of Mrs Daphne Negus, California.

Photograph: Margaret Rees

วิฬารเลิศพันธุ์   พรรณกาย

ขนด้วงดกหนาราย   เรียบร้อย

Left: Champion Wankee, the first recognized champion, from Simpson's Book of the Cat. And above: Harrison Weir, Founder of the British Cat Fancy.

Far left: **Mrs Robert Locke, U.S.A.** with **Calif, Siam and Bangkok** from Simpson's Book of the Cat. And left, from the same book: **Mummy of a cat in the British Museum.**

Photograph: Dr. B. R. Eustace

An early issue of "Fur and Feather"
August 28, 1890

One of the first cat shows,
with Frances Simpson and her steward.
From Simpson's Book of the Cat.

Female Korat, Double and International Champion. Cedar Glen's Ah So of Wila-Way. Owner Paul R. Bosley, Jr., Ohio. And below: Korat Male. Owner Merrill Tucker, New York. Both reproduced by courtesy of Mrs Daphne Negus, California.

Photograph: Anne Cumbers

Champion Ilowa Firefly. Red Point male. Owner Mrs White. And below: Doneraile Blue Penelope. The last cat bred by the late Kathleen Williams.

Photograph: Hugh Smith

Champion
Reegan Dessau.
Lilac Male.
Owner Mrs
Burlton.

Champion Sislinki Topsun.
Owner Mrs R. C. Hutton.

British bred Tabby Point, voted Miss Europe.
Owner Mrs Marx-Nielsen, Copenhagen.

Photograph: Anne Cumbers

Champion Amanda Rose.
Owner Mrs D. White.

Holliday's Margarita, an unusually beautiful American bred cat with many breeds in her pedigree. Breeder Ruthe K. Miner. Courtesy of Mrs Daphne Negus, California. And below: Champion White Tulip. Owner, Sam Scheer, U.S.A.

Photograph: Adriaanse, Holland

Far left: Premier Sukianga Cipollina, the first Tabby Point to win title. Owner Miss Moyse. Photograph Raymond Garnett. And left: Champion Katze Kim. First Irish bred Seal Point female to become a champion. Owner Mrs Maura Arthure.

Far left: Premier Chalmi Kayu. Owner Mrs Ann Imlach. Photograph Trygue Anderson.
And left: American Grand Champion Tuter's Black Bart. Owner Mrs Marge Naples. Photograph Victor Baldwin, California.

Stud Cat's beautifully constructed run, in splendid Scottish countryside. Owned by Mr & Mrs A. C. Saunders East Kilbride.

Far left: Premier Harcoosi Chui Chai. Blue Point. Owner Mrs Parkins. Photograph Antony Miles Ltd, Salisbury.
And left: First ever Siamese Grand Champion Tabby Point, Seremban Liger. Owner Mrs Anne Aslin.

Photograph: Joe Arce, U.S.A.

Napoleon. Jungle born and house trained.
Owner Rose Downing. Courtesy Mrs Daphne Negus, California.

First ever Siamese Grand Premier,
Karawong Taiwan
Owner/breeder Miss Fellows.

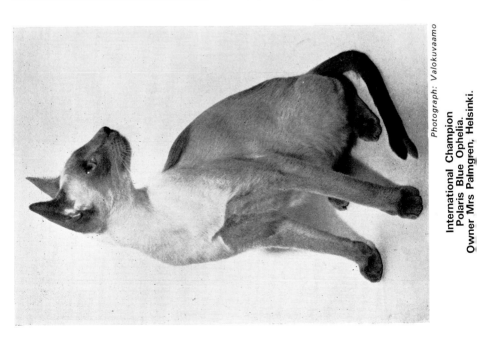

Photograph: Valokuvaamo

International Champion
Polaris Blue Ophelia.
Owner Mrs Palmgren, Helsinki.

swamping the Council. The first club inaugurated for
Siamese only, was the Siamese Cat Club, which for half
a century controlled the breeding, exhibiting, and the
general welfare of the Siamese. Then came the Siamese
Cat Society of the British Empire and the Siamese Cat
Association — two Southern clubs with changing
venues, but never venturing more than fifty miles from
London. The Northern Siamese and the Siamese Cat
Society of Scotland cater for Northern and Scottish
clubs. At these five shows Championships and Grand
Championships can be won. These clubs combine awards
for all varieties.

The surest way to inaugurate a new breed is to get
together a number of interested people, discuss everything about aspirations, hear each others' views and
there and then inaugurate a new club. Call it what you
like as long as it contains the name of the new breed or
variety, and all the founder members are breeders of the
new variety. Present it as a *fait accompli* to the Governing Council, and then things start happening.

For a real understanding of any new breed the first
priority is to be a breeder. Nothing is so important. The
planning of a litter, its arrival, its close inspection for
quality and quantity, its survival rate — all are noted by
a breeder dedicated to a new breed. If one owns both
sire and dam then this analysis must be very thorough
and searching. One wants to observe that the little
newcomers are miniatures of their parents, with no
obvious faults. This is observed with pleasure. They
should be a nice even litter of equal strength and stamina,
of nearly exact markings and points.

And the breeder, having bred her first litter to her
satisfaction, must go on and on until repetition is easy.
Other interested breeders could help a lot by keeping an
extra male for stud purposes. By close association they
will, between them, produce several generations of pure-

B

bred kittens. As soon as they are satisfied that type is right they will introduce the new breed to the Governing Council.

This is how things moved with Siamese. The various colour varieties are not new breeds but additional diversities to the well-established Siamese.

Turning back the pages once again, to nearly one hundred years ago, we read John Jennings', in his book *Domestic and Fancy Cats*, comment on experimentation:

> The Royal Cat of Siam can only be properly bred by crosses of its own variety. Experiments have been tried with a view to introducing another colour other than the characteristic dun, but, any deviation from the pure typical breed will, I opine, not be generally cared for, if for no other reason than its being incorrect.

Poor John! How things have changed! If you were alive today and saw what we now call Siamese you might like to change what you "opined" for when you first loved Siamese. We have now so many varieties in Siamese that they can fill a large show hall.

From the very beginning it was very difficult to separate the Seal Points from the Chocolate Points. These two colours were very much alike causing great confusion to breeders. Progress, and a more discerning fancier, amongst whom were some of our present-day judges, set themselves the task of establishing a club to look after the interests of Chocolate Points only, and a club was formed in 1954. They issued a standard of points which would distinguish the Chocolates as a separate variety for all time.

COLOUR, ACCORDING TO THE NEW STANDARDS

Points: Milk-chocolate colour, the ears, mask, legs, paws and tail to be the same colour, and the ears should not be darker in colour than the other points.

Eyes: Clear, bright, vivid blue.

Body: Ivory colour all over.

Everything else as for Seals.

From my experiences judging Siamese over a number of years I feel that it is not so easy to breed Chocolate champions. Even high class cats seem to be always waiting for something . . . waiting, all through the years for the mask to be complete, or for the brindling to clear on the front paws. Rarely, even when they have attained championship status, do they get full marks. For type and eye colour they are usually superb, but fail on mask, which should be complete, meaning that it should be connected by fine tracings with the ears. Very few Chocolate Points attain this perfection while young and they seem mostly to acquire it with age. They are the most beautiful of all varieties if they keep the ivory coat. Another difficulty is the attainment of *Milk* Chocolate Points. This is not a very clear description of colour, for there are people who never in their whole life have identified the colour, milk chocolate.

Phil Wade, one of the first writers to devote a whole book to Siamese, had plenty to say about another variety. These were the Blue Points. If ever a variety came unheralded it was this. Far away back in 1896 Louis Wain, acting as a judge, refused even to recognise a Blue Point exhibit at a show as Siamese. Certainly the first ones were freaks or sports because they came unheralded from Seal Point parents. Phil Wade, who was the Chairman of the Siamese Cat Club, was a person whose opinions mattered, and she did her best to put Blue Points right out. She never wanted them to compete with Seal Points. She wrote:

> Even the best blue-pointed cannot, I think, equal the beauty of our Seal-Pointed cats, and I can see no real object in trying to breed them. Their value at the moment is in their scarcity, but I cannot believe there will ever be a great demand for them.
>
> Let us concentrate on breeding perfect Siamese with deep Seal points, long, wedge-shaped heads, and marvellous blue oriental-shaped eyes. We can never better that quite lovely colour scheme.

But not all fanciers thought alike. Certainly the name "Blue" was an attractive variation, and the Blue Point Cat Club founded in 1944 set out very pleasing standards. The club tried to give the coat colour a distinctly new nomenclature. We had Seal Points with cream body coat shading gradually into pale warm fawn, Chocolates with body colour ivory all over, Blue Points with glacial white coats. These beautiful varieties had clubs to look after their interests and it was not until twenty years later that the Seal Pointed cats got a club of their own. But in the intervening years the three known varieties were bred with each other. Some fanciers agree that the indiscriminate matings of Seal Points and Blue Points had already done untold damage to the Seal Points.

There are many breeders who attribute the loss of the glacial white coat to the introduction of Seal Points into the breeding in the same way as more and more breeders say the deterioration of the colour of the coat in Seal Points is the direct result of mixed breeding. A few years ago a Seal Point Cat Club was founded. This was to help the Seal Points breeding with great emphasis on coat colour but we have yet to see the light coat return to the Seal Points. Undoubtedly they have beautiful types today, but the coat colour is no longer "cream, shading gradually into pale fawn on the back". That is an image of the past, we, of this generation, will never see again. Today there is a recklessness about indiscriminate breeding that is hard to ignore.

Then, almost head and heel on top of the Blue Points we get another variety, Lilac Points. There is something strikingly beautiful about these cats, especially if they appear in numbers at shows. They have a few distinctive features outlined in their standards of points. Points should be pinkish grey, nose leather and pads faded lilac. Body colour is off-white, magnolia to be precise, and the eyes should be clear, bright vivid blue. Unlike the Blue

Points they keep their off-white coats for life. Lilac Points need more show preparation than any of the other varieties because if neglected their coat can appear very dingy. To attain championships they must be spotless in every detail. Many breeders think they have overtaken the Blue Points in popularity; again, in my judging experience I would say "not quite". Although the Blues have lost their glacial white coat, they have gained in type. There are some magnificent specimens of both varieties to be seen at shows today. Mrs. Carol Stafford's Grand Champion, Kaprico Iceberg, bred on Tyne and Wear is the most beautiful Lilac Point ever exhibited.

Judging cats on colour only can lead one into many pitfalls. Colour is a varying thing and can alter from month to month or from season to season. Type is the thing that matters for it rarely alters during the life time of a healthy cat.

The four varieties, Seal-pointed, Chocolate-pointed, Blue-pointed and Lilac-pointed, completed a nice cycle and brought great interest to Siamese breeders. Each was perfect in its way. They were all Siamese, with the same characteristics. It looked as if they were a great happy family with few differences. They got the breed numbers, 24, for Seal-points and with the addition of a, b, c, the other varieties came into line. It was very satisfying to breeders to see how easily they fell into step.

Then something new appeared. A perfect Siamese with tabby markings, restricted only to points. They were first seen on exhibition in 1962 at the Croydon Cat Show. Crowds gathered round the pens all day, asking questions. Even as small kittens they had excellent type. The first litter was said to have been brought about through the mating of a short hair tabby with the Seal Point Siamese. The experts immediately recognised that they had something good. They were adopted by fanciers with a flair for the exquisite in animal and man and, by trying many variations in breeding, the perfect Tabby Point arrived. This time the people concerned knew that there were more changes in the offing and insisted on getting a new number — 32. The standard agreed was:

Body Colour:	Pale coat preferably free from markings, and conforming to recognised standards for Siamese.
Ears:	Solid, no stripes, thumb mark.
Nose Leather:	Again conforming to recognised standards for the particular colour of the points.
Mask:	Clearly defined stripes, especially round the eyes and nose. Distinct markings on cheeks, darkly spotted whisker pads.
Eyes:	Brilliant clear blue. The lids dark-rimmed or toning with the points.
Legs:	Varied sized broken stripes, solid markings on back of hind legs.
Tail:	Varied sized clearly defined rings ending in a solid patch.

The Tabby Points got away with a good start. Mrs. Warner's Champion Spotlight Kopeika, paraded before us — a Tabby Point debutante of such exquisite beauty that her judges were breathless when trying to describe her. She won all the way from kittenhood to adulthood and was a fine specimen to demonstrate a new breed. Her superb head shape and eye colour have never been surpassed. She set up a great race to championship honours and left so many "also rans" that breeders were asking, "However has she done it?" She demonstrated the "thumb mark" on her ear and equalled the standards as no other Tabby Point has done before or since.

So now it was the turn of the Red Points and they made immediate headway, and were given the breed number of 32a. This variety was shown for many years under breed number 26, Any Other Variety. They had very good breeding behind them and entered the show scene already made up for championship status. Like the Tabby Points their first and important characteristic quality was that they were to be Siamese in type, head shape, eyes and ears, and strong chin according to standards. The body colour should be white, shading, if any, to apricot on the back. Their points should be of bright reddish gold. Aesthetically they have few rivals in the cat world. Here, as with the Tabby Points, they got away with a good start. What we saw first exhibited were pleasing beyond description, and they have improved with the passing of time. In the North of England cats bred under the prefix, "Darling" owned by Mrs. George have set the seal on beauty as applied to cats. Grand Champion Darling Red Shadow owned by Mrs. Deakin won the American "Cat World" award for supreme Best Cat of the 1974-75 season.

Still in the 32 bracket, this time come the Torties (Tortoishells) registered by the number 32b. These have the markings of the ordinary British Tortie cat, but in Siamese Tortie Points the markings are restricted to the mask, ears, nose, tail, legs. A spread of markings all over the back is a serious fault. In type they must be true Siamese, with the wedge-shaped head, oriental blue eyes, and whipped tail. The origin of the breed has been difficult to trace, but Mrs. Lucy Price's (a well-known judge and breeder) statement is most probably the correct answer — a miss-mating with Seal Point and an ordinary red Tabby, and amongst the resultant kittens was a Tortie of Siamese type. The Red Points crossed with other varieties have continued to produce Torties. Being female only they can never mate with a cat of their own variety, but are very useful in a breeding programme. Sometimes they arrive accidentally and sometimes by design.

Tortie Points are now well established. There is no doubt that Torties, as we know them today, are Siamese Tortie Points and could not pass for any other breed. At first the Torties we saw at shows lacked Siamese type and had not the markings restricted to their points. They were also very round in the head.

Since the new varieties have been recognised and championships been awarded they have increased enormously in popularity and very full classes appear at all the shows. As Seal Points and Blue Points have been crossed successfully with each other, so the crossing of the old and new varieties produces good results. The late Mrs. Elsie Kent, one of the most well-known and important of Siamese judges of our day, wrote in *Fur and Feather:*

> Referring to litters which appeared at the Kensington Show 1969. Most of the litters were mixtures of Blue, Lilac, Chocolate, Seal and Tortie. Anyone, especially a novice, would have no idea of what their adults will produce unless they know all the cats in all the pedigrees. What a pity this state of affairs has been allowed to arise! A breeder would be lucky today to find a sire and dam guaranteed to throw a litter of all one colour.

These comments were welcomed, but did nothing to slow down the stampede of breeding all varieties mixed up together. The 1970's saw very many odd-looking Siamese, and they became the subjects of much experimental breeding, not always to the good.

The Tabby Points can be mated to Seal, Blue, Chocolate and Lilac, though the Seal-pointed Tabby Point has not been equalled. And the same thing can be done with the Torties, and here again, the most distinctive Tortie is a Seal Tortie. Experiments have produced many more varieties, like Blue Cream and Lilac Cream, and Chocolate Cream Torties.

Cream as a distinct variety has now been recognised, and can attain Championship status. This cat can be registered under the number 32c. Again, we are presented with a beautiful Siamese whose standard of points varies little from the Red Points, except that we insert the word Cream where we formerly had the word Red. Mrs. Margaret Baxter, who worked so hard for the recognition of Creams, described them poetically and affectionately as:

The Creams, like the Lilacs, are so pretty, with their white bodies faintly flushed, their eyes so strongly and brightly blue, and their softly pinky beige points, and their nature so loving, and happy and easy.

Many breeds originated from Siamese. The Burmese was established in America before it was brought into England. It is definite that it arrived in America about 1930, and after much experimentation in which Siamese were used in matings with a self brown short hair cat, a Brown Burmese cat was evolved. These were imported to England by Mr. and Mrs. France in 1949. They did not take long to achieve recognition, and soon became a very popular breed. Further experimentation has now brought in all varieties of colour, and these are very attractive cats.

The Havana, first named Chestnut Brown Foreign, is another English manufactured breed in which crosses with Siamese and plain black coated cats were brought into existence. These did not achieve immediate popularity, possibly on account of their resemblance to other short hair breeds. Now, largely through the persistence and dedication of some fanciers, they are appearing on the show bench in increased numbers.

But the Siamese has a rather distinguished role to play in matters feline, for so many of the older breeds have stolen from him his two toned colouring, and even his sparkling blue eyes. Even the majestic Persians or Long Hairs, with so much beauty already theirs, were not content with being just pure white, or cream, or blue, but had to inveigle the Siamese into their breeding cycle and capture the much coveted two tone markings. The late Brian Stirling Webb saw the beauty of a Long-Haired Siamese, and in the early fifties started his experimentation. Mrs. J. P. Harding perfected what Stirling Webb started, and now we have Colourpoints in the same variety of colours as the Siamese. But the breeders of

Colourpoints disown any correlation with Siamese. In colour and point marking only is there any affinity. The eyes of the Colourpoints must be round and full, while Siamese eyes are the reverse. Also in type they adhere to the standards for Long Hairs. In fact, any resemblance but colour is a serious fault.

The most positively distinct breed of this era has been the Rex, the name given to the curly-coated cat. The cat statisticians report that this mutation occurs only once in a million but, knowing that all sorts of oddities appear from time to time in the domestic cat, it can be assumed that there is a higher ratio but that the curls have not been observed. There are two varieties, the Devon and the Cornish, and now the Si-Rex. This last variety was created by bringing in the Siamese to the Rex breeding programme. It was a pity to do this at such an early stage as they had not really established the Rex cat to everyone's liking. The Si-Rex is not a beautiful cat as he is neither one thing or another.

Another striking newcomer is the Foreign White. He has been carefully bred with many important fanciers in at his birth. He is, in fact, a White Siamese. If one wants beauty around the house, bring in the Foreign White.

For breeding purposes Seal Points are the undenied progenitors of all that is best in the Siamese cat. The first Colourpoint, the Havana, the first Burmese, the first Tabby Point, the first Foreign White and the first Si-Rex, were all directly related to the Seal Point. In fact the breeding policy of the Foreign White Group urged that Seal Point Siamese should be used as the coloured mates whenever possible.

And so the story goes. Breeders seem to be clutching at the Siamese as to a sinking ship. There is no escape for him. All the way along the line his beauty has been coveted by the big and the little, by the great and the small.

4. The Siamese Cat becomes a Show Cat

The first cat show was organised by Harrison Weir and was held at the Crystal Palace in 1871, and cat shows have been held since with only the breaks caused by world wars. The National Cat Club ruled the Fancy without dispute until 1898 when there was a split in its ranks and the "Cat Club" was formed, but after a few years the "Cat Club" too came to an end and the National Cat Club once again took over the reins of government. The Club was well run and had a strict code of morals, even to the keeping of a "black list". People in this list had been guilty, as members or otherwise, of fraudulent or discreditable behaviour in regard to cats and cat shows. These people would not be countenanced by the National Cat Club in any capacity.

However, Harrison Weir was more than elated about the success of his first show. In his book, *Our Cats and All About Them,* he described the event:

> On the day for judging, at Ludgate Hill, I took a ticket and the train for the Crystal Palace. Sitting alone in the comfortable compartment of a "first class", I confess I felt somewhat more than anxious as to the issue of the experiment. Yes; what would it be like? Would there be many cats? How many?

43

How would the animals comport themselves in their cages?
Would they sulk or cry for liberty? refuse all food? or settle
down and take the situation quietly and resignedly or give
way to terror? I could in no way picture to myself the scene;
it was all so new. Presently, and while I was musing on the
subject the door opened and a friend got in. "Ah" said he
"how are you?" "Tolerably well," said I; "I am on my way to
the Cat Show." "What" said my friend, "that surpasses everything! A show of cats! Why, I hate the things; I drive them off
my premises when I see them. You'll have a fine bother with
them in their cages! Or are they to be tied up? Anyway, what
a noise there will be, and how they will clutch at the bars and
try to get out, or they will strangle themselves with their
chains." "I am sorry, very sorry," said I "that you do not like
cats. For my part I think they are extremely beautiful, also very
graceful in their actions, and they are quite as domestic in
their habits as the dog, if not more so. They are very useful in
catching rats and mice; they are not deficient in sense; they
will jump up at doors to push up latches with their paws. I
have known them knock at a door by the knocker and
wanting admittance. They know Sunday from the week-day,
and they do not go out to wait for the meat barrow on that
day; they . . ." "Stop" said my friend, "I see you do like cats,
and I do not, so let the matter drop." "No," said I "not so.
This is why I instituted the Cat Show; I wish everyone to see
how beautiful a well-cared-for cat is and how docile, gentle,
and — may I use the term — cossety. Why should not the cat
that sits purring in front of us before the fire be an object of
interest, and be selected for its colour, markings, and form?
Now come with me, my dear old friend, and see the first Cat
Show."

Inside the Crystal Palace stood my friend and I. Instead of
the noise and struggles to escape, there lay the cats in their
different pens, reclining on crimson cushions, making no
sound save now and then a homely purring, as from time to
time they lapped the nice new milk provided for them. Yes,
there they were, big cats, very big cats, middling-sized cats,
and small cats, cats of all colours and markings, and beautiful
pure white persians, and as we passed down the front of the
cages I saw that my friend became interested; presently he
said: "What a beauty this is! and here's another!" "And no
doubt," said I, "many of the cats you have seen before would
be quite as beautiful if they were well cared for, or at least
cared for at all; generally they are driven about and ill-fed,
and often ill-used, simply for the reason that they are cats,
and no other. Yet I feel a great pleasure in telling you the show
would have been much larger were it not for the difficulty of

inducing the owners to send their pets from home though you see the great care that is taken of them." "Well, I had no idea that there was such a variety of form, size and colour" and he said Goodbye and departed.

A few months later, I called on him; he was at luncheon, with two cats on a chair beside him — pets, I should say, from their appearance. This is not a solitary instance of the good of the first Cat Show leading up to the observation of, and kindly feeling for, the domestic cat.

The newly inaugurated Cat Fancy now with something definite in mind, set about studying and identifying the various breeds of cat that hitherto had no names or classification. Persians, already appraised for beauty and elegance, were soon to be singled out for special breed numbers. This was done, at first, on colour variations. Blue Persians had many admirers, and breeders could separate them from other breeds. Many of the leisured rich adopted the Blue Persian, sometimes called the Archangel Cat, and started a breeding programme.

Under the heading, Points of Excellence, Harrison Weir set out his standards of points for all the various colours in Long Hairs. The White Persian was a great favourite of his. Here is an extract which detailed his findings:

> Head: Round and broad across and between the eyes, of medium size; nose rather short, pink at the tip; ears ordinary size, but looking small, being surrounded with long hair, which should also be long on the forehead. Eyes: Large, full round or almond-shape, lustrous, and of a beautiful azure blue. Yellow admissible as five points only. Green a defect.

An intelligible standard of points was set for all the cats that had come up for approbation. Attention was given to ruff, fur, frill, tail, size, shape and condition and points were allotted for each. If it were possible to find two or three cats alike from the same cattery, they were especially welcomed and might even end up with getting a breed number. In colour varieties, we had, in addition to Blue and White, Blacks, Tortoiseshells, Reds, Yellows,

Tabbies, Light Greys, Dark Greys and many others.

Then the short-haired cats were considered. In this category, the Tabby Cat got great prominence. Harrison Weir set a very high standard for the distribution of markings, which read:

> Jet-black lines, not too broad, scarcely so wide as the ground colour shown between, so as to give a light and brilliant effect. When the black lines are broader than the colour space it is a defect, being then black marked with colour, instead of colour marked with black. The lines must be clear, sharp, and well-defined, in every way distinct, having no mixture of the ground colour. Head and legs marked regularly, the rings on the throat and chest being in no way blurred or broken, but clear, graceful and continuous; lips, cushions of feet, and the backs of hind-legs, and the ear-points, black.

To a non-fancier, these details might appear absurd or even laughable, but not to a serious breeder. Harrison Weir was nothing if he were not thorough. He took his new task seriously. He was a dedicated cat show organiser. The pedigree cat was particularly welcomed if he came with a title. In this category were the Abyssinians and Manx.

Then, to the lasting benefit of the Siamese cat, he arrived in Britain just in time to take his place at the first shows. His coming was simultaneous with the inauguration of the Cat Fancy. After very careful study the standards for the Royal Cat of Siam were set out as follows:

> Head:
> Small, broad across and between the eyes, tapering upwards and somewhat narrow between the ears; forehead flat and receding, nose long, and somewhat broad, cheeks narrowing towards the mouth, lips full and rounded, ears rather large and wide at base, with very little hair inside.   10 points
>
> Fur:
> Very short and somewhat woolly, yet soft and silky to the touch, and glossy, with much lustre on the face, legs and tail.
>   10 points.

Colour:

The ground or body colour to be of an even tint, slightly darker on the back, but not in any way clouded or patched with any darker colour; light rich dun is the preferable colour, but a light fawn, light silver-grey, or light orange is allowable: deeper and richer browns, almost chocolate, are admissible if even and not clouded, but the first is the true type, the last merely a variety of much beauty and excellence: but the dun and light take preference.   20 points.

Markings:

Ears black, the colour not extending beyond them, but ending in a clear and well-defined outline: around the eyes, and all the lower part of the head, black: legs and tail black, the colour not extending into or staining the body, but having a clear line of demarcation.   20 points.

Eyes:

Rather of almond shape, slanting towards the nose, full and a very beautiful blue opalesque in colour, luminous and of a reddish tint in the dusk of evening or artificial light.

15 points.

Tail:

Short by comparison with the English cat, thin throughout, a little thicker towards the base, without any break or kink.

5 points.

Size and Form:

Rather small, lithe, elegant in outline; legs thin and a little short than otherwise; feet long, not so round as the ordinary cat; neck long and small.   10 points.

Condition:

In full health, not too fat, hair smooth, clear, bright, full of lustre, lying close to the body, which should be hard and firm in the muscles.   10 points.

Total   100 points.

It was clear to see how much time and thought Harrison Weir had given to determining the standards for Siamese, and the standards written above were a true photostat of the Siamese as he saw them. After the establishment of the Siamese Cat Club in 1902 standards were altered to be more easily adapted to the popular cat of the day. Body colour "as light and even as possible, cream being the most desirable". Seal brown was decided to be a better description of the points, than black. The "marten" look was introduced into the standard of points. This was a difficult analogy as few breeders had ever seen a marten and the dictionary analysis was simply "Animal like a weasel, with valuable fur". However the word "marten" must have appealed as it stuck almost to the present day.

During the first decade of the Siamese show cat's existence there was much controversy between breeders. The Seal Point and the Chocolate Point fought hard for a separate existence, and the Siamese Cat Club tried to encourage breeders to keep them separate. The "kink" in the tail, always appearing in new litters, was frowned on though the first British champion, Wankee, owned by Mrs. Robinson, a member of the Siamese Cat Club and a well-known judge, had a pronounced "kink". At that time the question of kinks was a matter on which the Siamese Cat Club remained neutral.

There is fashion in everything. With humans, there are hair styles, make-up, clothes à la Paris or London cut, colour schemes, figures and physiques, footwear, speech, and many more things which stamp us as being in the fashion. Fashionable folk belong to uppercrust society. Animals too have their own high status, and Siamese cats, in particular, have become the fashionable cats of today. For a long time now, the scales have been tilted in their favour and they are the acknowledged top cat of the seventies. For brief periods new breeds have been adopted. Cat clubs have been created for their inauguration of standards and introduction to the public. But sometimes their appeal has not been sustained when their popularity wanes. Plain, self-coloured cats have little interest to the camera man, while the two tone markings and the glorious blue eyes of the Siamese mark him straight away as a cat with a difference. On coloured television he is superb.

There are, however, some whose loyalties would

always veer towards Long Hairs, and the beauty of the Persian can never be questioned. Comparison between

THE CHANGING FACE OF THE SIAMESE CAT
1924   1977

Long Hairs and others is summed up beautifully by Katherine L. Simms, a cat lover of distinction of the early fifties, in her book *They Walked Beside Me:*

> Notice how the nether garments of the different sorts of cats vary. The hind legs of the Long Hair are clad in a feathery effect of baggy Moslem pantaloons caught in at the ankles. The half-breed wears jodhpurs, wide at the top and slim of leg. The Short Hair appears always in theatrical tights.

In every country in the world today, ownership of a Siamese cat carries with it a fashionable tone, which is seldom associated with the other varieties. During my recent visit to Canada, this idea of mine was confirmed. Mixing socially with many Canadians, I was delighted to find how many of them kept Siamese as pets. In the remote part of Saskatchewan where I stayed, cat shows had not made much impact. Cat owners were happy to be apprised of all details about cat shows. All the big cities in Canada have their annual shows. In 1974, Regina held its first for pedigree cats. It was sponsored by a newly inaugurated cat club, calling itself The Prairie Lily Cat Club of which I am a member.

There is a very close affinity between the registering bodies of the American and Canadian fanciers, and vast distances between them present no problems. Cats can be shown in both countries, carrying their honours with them. The great continent of Australia also bids welcome to pedigree cats, with Siamese once again the star performer. Many breeders, now with a very extensive breeding programme of many feline varieties, will readily admit that the first pedigree cat they ever owned was a Siamese.

Mrs. Marge Naples, writing in 1964, *This is the Siamese Cat*, did much for American bred Siamese. Apart from the excellent guidance and direction it gave about the show cat, it had so much fun contained within its pages that no one could ignore it. A chapter on Cat Clothes was a masterpiece of sly humour. Dressing up the cat in Yankee style was fun, but dressing up father in matching garments — a sweater featuring a Blue Point Siamese, accompanied by a pair of socks, also to blend with other extras — made ecstatic reading. It would certainly make a cat laugh!

Writing to me for inclusion in my book Marge said:

I do not need to tell anyone that Siamese are great cats. Their personality as well as their striking looks win people over before they know it. I have been working with them since 1954, and showed my first one in 1958. I still have his Best Novice Rosette he won at the show.

For those interested in shows an understanding of the terminology is important.

Our interpretation of "Foreign" is as follows:

Cats of foreign type should be fine in bone, lithe and sinuous and with graceful proportions. Heads are long and pointed and ears are sharp, large and broad at the base. The tail is long and for some breeds, whipped, and oriental eyes give the desired "foreign" look. Coat should be short and glossy, varying in colour, according to the breed named.

The recognition of Foreign Short Hairs has brought glamour and interest into cat breeding. An astute judge of cats could almost single out type by feeling alone. It is only when the breeds are crossed that definition becomes difficult.

The competition in cat shows helps to establish the type, colour and overall appearance of the cats we wish to perpetuate. The judges make their nominations and champions are created. Though many beautiful cats never make the grade, we still must look to the certificated for determining our own standards. Every show season finishes with publication of the names of cats, their owners and their breeders which have become champions and premiers during the year. Considering the rapid growth in pedigree cat breeding and the ever-swelling numbers appearing at shows, the list of champions is very small.

The shows of the old days were very different from ours of today. Cats were given special tuition as to how to behave. In Frances Simpson's book she wrote unblushingly:

> Cats require to be educated to the show pen, and it is necessary in some cases to give a course of training. For this purpose it is well to obtain a similar pen to those used at shows and to place your puss in this for an hour or two daily. In time he will learn to come and sit and look out of his temporary prison, and when he makes his debut he will not spoil his chances by crouching at the back of the show pen, or vex his would-be admirers who may have recourse to the use of an umbrella or stick to make the exhibit move into a more convenient and conspicuous position.

These tactics would not be tolerated today, nevertheless they are worth considering. Sometimes at our shows cats are encouraged by their owners to conceal themselves under the blanket. This can be an annoyance, preventing the judge from giving the exhibits the final look over. This habit should be discouraged as, when dealing with breeding queens, many kittens are smothered by the protective attitude of the mother. The ideal set-up is for the cat to be visible from top to toe, reclining on a nice warm blanket exuding contentment. If he has to be taken out he is not so resentful as the cat swathed in woollies. Many exhibitors break the rules by dressing up the cat too much. One warm blanket should be enough.

There are three kinds of shows, all of which are run under Governing Council rules. The first show a club runs is called an *Exemption* of trial show. The second is a *Sanction* show, almost a Championship show. The third is a *Championship* show at which championships and premierships can be won.

Grooming a Siamese for a show is very easy compared to grooming Long Hairs. Only if a Siamese gets into trouble outside should a complete bath be necessary. The easiest and most effective way of beautifying your Siamese is to clean his fur like a furrier does, by using bran. This should be slightly dampened and rubbed in all over, especially in concealed parts. When brushed out it gives a nice sheen to the coat. This should be repeated a few times. Attention should always be given to the extremities. Ears in particular should be cleaned with a little cotton wool dipped in spirit, or even with ordinary soap, which must be well washed out. If there is any suspicion of ear mites the exhibit should be withdrawn from competition. White hairs on the mask or round the eyes are a sign of recent illness. This is called "brindling".

As written in the schedule the pen appurtenances must be white, with no distinguishing mark anywhere. A hot water bottle makes for contentment, and should be concealed under the blanket. Drinking water is allowed in the pen but no food during the judging.

The veterinary surgeon will testify to the cat's good health, and each exhibit will be given an All-clear. Nothing should be round the neck of the exhibit but the pen number on a white tape or elastic. Dainty ribbons with bows are forbidden. The cat should never be left without a toilet tray; litter is supplied by show organisers.

Attention must also be given to the judges. Note his or her name. To become a champion a cat has to meet three different judges and win a first prize under each. It is said that certain judges only like certain cats of certain type. This is quite wrong. All judges like good type, but there may be some slight deviations in the final assessment.

Be a good loser; cat showing is only a hobby, and should be an enjoyable one.

For the novice or newcomer to showing, there must be before his mind a few of the essentials for point scoring, without which his cat could not be called a show cat. A Siamese cat should be of medium build, muscular and with a good length of body. Cobbiness is a fault. The head will be wedge shaped, and modern trends are for long heads. Eyes should be blue, different depth in colour for the different varieties. Tail should be long and whipped. The distribution of the colour, which gives the name to the variety, should be restricted to points only (viz. nose and part of face, ears, tail and legs) and body colour should be unmarked. Foreign type is the same for all the varieties. Cats should be presented for exhibition in an absolutely flawless condition, sparklingly clean, well groomed, and in perfect health. Anonymity is essential.

Exhibitors should be cognisant of all show rules and regulations which are published in the schedule. They should know exactly what they are looking for. The word CHAMPION has a magic ring all its own. To become a champion a cat must have three challenge certificates, signed by three different judges, at three championship shows. To become a grand champion the same procedure is followed. Neuters can become premiers and grand premiers just the same way as entire cats.

The Secretary of the Governing Council of the British Cat Fancy, whose name and address is below:

Mrs. W. Davey,
Dovefields,
Petworth Road, Witley, Surrey

will help all fanciers with any inquiries about pedigree cats. Inquiries should be accompanied by a stamped, addressed envelope.

The schedule is sent to club members by the show manager, enclosing a list of rules and the entry form. The correct filling in of the entry form is a very necessary piece of show procedure and should be carefully studied. Be sure the cat is properly registered and transferred (if you have not bred it). Age is important, for a kitten cannot be entered in as an adult cat until it is nine months old. Study the open class which caters for your particular variety, and you will have great joy if you win any of the other classes. These are breeders, novice, maiden class, novices and the club classes. Many show managers do not pay prize money for open classes but present rosettes. There are usually many special prizes to be won, and the practice of paying out money on side classes on the show day is now almost universal. It is nice to go home without an empty pocket as well as having had a good day at the show.

Show costs today are astronomical; it is a wonder they can keep going. Exhibitors, too, are finding things almost out of their reach. Long and tedious rail and car journeys add up to tremendous cash outlay. Still, fanciers in search of honours for their beloved cats never count the cost. To bring home a champion is the final accolade. Well do I remember my own showing days with pride and joy and the rush to the nearest post office to send a telegram with the happy news:

Sig, First and Champion!

An Example of a Champion's Pedigree. It belongs to Champion Kaloke Fingal, bred by Mrs. M. Key.

Parents	Grand-Parents	Great-Grand-Parents	Great-Great-Grand-Parents
Sire CHAMPION Dezna Cometes 5 C.C.s	Sire CHAMPION Kuala Caru 24	Sire CHAMPION Siepoo Storm 24	Sire Kuala Igai 24 / Dam CHAMPION Silken Philylla 24
		Dam CHAMPION Karawong Amaryllis 24	Sire Kuala Exorchorda 24 1 C.C. / Dam Kuala Blue Banka 24A
	Dam CHAMPION Roundway Quince 24	Sire CHAMPION Sabukia Sirocco 24	Sire CHAMPION Killdown Kerry 24 / Dam CHAMPION Sabukia Saina 24
		Dam CHAMPION Roundway Jonquil 24	Sire CHAMPION Bolney Kien 24B / Dam Roundway Chelone 24
Dam CHAMPION Kaloke Fingal 4 C.C.s 24	Sire GRAND CHAMPION Kaloke Pharaoh (4 Gr.Ch's) 24	Sire CHAMPION Sabukia Sirocco 24	Sire CHAMPION Killdown Kerry 24 / Dam CHAMPION Sabukia Saina 24
		Dam Cymbeline Chemeli 24	Sire CHAMPION Marshbrook Kwando 24 / Dam CHAMPION Dunchattan Ayshah 24
	Dam Kaloke Farah 2 C.C.s 24	Sire CHAMPION Sabukia Sirocco 24	Sire CHAMPION Killdown Kerry 24 / Dam CHAMPION Sabukia Saina 24
		Dam Twislehope Sadiya 24	Sire Crimplesham Saki 24 / Dam Pennyhope 24

5. The Siamese becomes a Pet Cat

Puss Puss!
— Oh Auntie, isn't he a beauty? And is he a gentleman or a lady?
— Neither, my dear! I had him fixed. It saves him from so many undesirable associations.

(D. H. Lawrence)

While the creators of the newly established Cat Fancy were busy measuring, tabulating, illustrating, registering, approving, naming, setting out standards, and putting Siamese through their paces, quite a few cats managed to break away, and settle for no shows, no disciplines, and snuggle into the arms of a human being, giving and expecting only love in return. These were the pet cats and were mostly neuters. These were the cats of the good life.

Many pet lovers went to great lengths to acquire this cat with a difference. The first Siamese to have had a book written all to himself was Charles O'Malley. He was the friend and companion of writer and publisher Michael Joseph. Charles was lucky to have had such a master, and the Siamese breed was lucky to have had such a boost from a cat lover, who had known so many non-pedigree cats and had found none of them wanting. But about Charles, there was no mistake. In him Michael Joseph found his greatest companion. In later years Sir John Smythe presented to the reading public his *Beloved Cats* which were at first always Siamese. Later he introduced Burmese into his happy family of cats.

The Incredible Journey, written by Sheila Burnford, was the most outstanding animal story of the age. The "incredible" journey, over "a vast area of deeply wooded wilderness — of endless chains of lonely lakes and rushing rivers" had for its leader, Tao, the little Siamese cat. Doreen Tovey's *Cats in the Belfrey* set up a chain of lightly-written enjoyable stories about Siamese and their ways, that promoted Siamese out of their unfounded reputation as rather dour and distant-mannered cats, to being jolly, gay and companionable above all other breeds. These books are a riot of laughter. Many other books of the past decade helped to establish certain qualities in Siamese that have endeared them to humans. As far as I can remember, others who have written lovingly of the Siamese cat are Katherine L. Simms — *These I Have Loved*, Katherine M. Abbott — *Cat Enchanted*, and Pamela and James Mason in *The Cats in our Lives*. Then there were many practical books written by modern writers.

The practice of neutering cats came down to us from the Victorian age. As cats were the much adored companions of the greatest ladies in the land their devotion to their owner had to be all-embracing. Entire males presented too many olfactory annoyances, and females could be embarrassing by a constant arrival of kittens. So it had to be that cats with an entrée to high society were deprived of their natural functions. The popularizing of neutering had an immediate effect on establishing the house pet cat.

It was generally agreed that neutering had no ill effects; on the contrary neutered cats retained their beauty and, being stronger since neutering, were more comfortable to live with. Their characters too became more mellow and they were more affectionate and docile than their undoctored kin. Personality changes were observed in the Victorian cats. From being shy and unobtrusive a neutered cat suddenly became forward and full of bounce, relinquishing his seat in the porch or the back kitchen for the best chair in the drawing room. Mrs. Prescott, the American nineteenth-century novelist, always brought cats into her writing. Talking about her six-toed neuter and a strange idiosyncrasy he had developed since neutering, she wrote:

> Now Lucifer sucks his tail, alas! and alas! In vain have we peppered it, and pepper-sauced it, and dipped it in Worcester sauce and in aloes, and done it up in papers, and glued on to it the fingers of old gloves. At last we gave it up in despair, and I took him and put his tail into his mouth, and told him to take his pleasure, and that is the reason I suppose, he attached himself to me.

And for the past hundred years neutered cats came into our lives and we loved them for their idiosyncrasies. A Siamese neuter suddenly develops a personality. If he is neutered while young many attractive traits in his character will surely develop.

Zaida, the then well-known cat columnist in the early editions of *Fur and Feather*, wrote in 1901 notes urging the practice of neutering:

> "For a perfect household pet the neuter cats holds its own. Too often the purchaser of a kitten starts breeding and multiplying a race of weedy, ill-kept animals who do not do much credit to their owner. A cat with kittens in undoubtedly a charming sight but a female cat is more or less a worry, and is never in condition for showing. Then a tomcat roams, fights and is often objectionable, but the stay-at-home cat is always a thing of beauty and a great companion of the hearth."

So it was then, and now many of the most important of all pet cats are neuters. The adored pets of the ladies of the lonely hearts are invariably neuters, and the cats that make the headlines in poetry and prose, in music and song, are neuters.

Many things have been written about Siamese cats. One of the truest and most incontestable is that a Siamese cat is an animal of character. It is easier to understand what character means if one is conversant with things in reverse order, as applied to humans. A person without character is described as characterless — ordinary, undistinguished, without testimonial. None of those adjectives can apply to the Siamese cat. He is not ordinary, undistinguished or without testimonial. Every owner of a Siamese cat will agree that he has an abundance of virtues. When he comes into your home, it will never be the same again. It may seem as if some transcendental being has invaded it. Suddenly something has pleasantly disturbed the even tenor of your life. You are alone no more.

'Why do you love me?' the little kitten asks its new owner. After the first few days of isolation from its own kith and kin, it has finally found you and decided that you are his. Henceforth, all his love and devotion is yours. He knows you love him too, and thus his plea: 'Why do you love me?'

You love him because he is an exquisite, lovable little creature. If in good health, he exudes charm. He is delightful to look at and heavenly to hold. At a very early age the characteristics of his forbears begin to show themselves.

Even in dealing with cats, comparisons are odious, and so I hesitate to place the Siamese on a pedestal of his own. Nevertheless, experience tells us that the Persian is a proud cat and very class conscious. Unless he were a fool he could not fail to be impressed by the care taken of his appearance and the never ending grooming. He knows he is somebody in the cat world. His manners are rather aloof, especially to strangers. Many of the Short Hair cats, including British ones, are indistinguishable in manners. The foreign cats alone are different and in this category come the Siamese.

Now here is a friend indeed. There is nothing you can do that he cannot do better. When it is walking out time for humans, it will also be walking out time for your Siamese. He can outrun the greatest human sprinter. My first Siamese cat, old Ming, even in later life when almost as deaf as a doorpost and very nearly blind too, never missed an opportunity to walk with me in the garden. She seemed to sense movement. In those days we had a sizable garden — a walk in it really was a walk! Crazy paving paths were bordered by box hedges, which were growing so tall and intertwined together that if Ming did not keep to the paths she would lose me. She had to tread warily, as jumping in the dark was completely beyond her ken. 'Old age,' mused Ming, 'must be dignified, even in cats.'

Inquisitiveness is another trait almost peculiar to the Siamese. They never give up. Delivery of a large box, packet or container will set his nerves on edge. He will not relax until he has found out what is inside it. Nor does he easily forget. Old Ming associated lean and hungry days with an unpleasant kennel, and the dusting of our old family trunk immediately sent her into hiding. Ming hated her separation from me and the restricted life she had had to lead. In fact, the memory of her one and only visit to boarding kennels left such a nasty taste in her mouth that she would think of any kind of ruse to avoid the same fate and prison fare.

A Siamese is an unusual cat in so far as he will try to guard your home. If there is no man in the house, a Siamese cat can take on a watch dog role. Any strange sound can impel him to growl like a dog and he can adopt a very truculent attitude if he intends to threaten. He is a quick change artist too. He can suddenly turn on the charm act and look for the knee of his best beloved, before taking his afternoon nap. And if the leaves of a book block his view of the fire, then he has been known to turn over the pages. When the day's work is done, there is no situation so happy for a cat lover than to pull up close to the fire, with his Siamese pet lying across his knee.

A Siamese cat is an interesting, unusual creature, with a certain something not found in many other domestic animals. Beneath the surface of the Siamese lies a tempestuous nature which he has learned to control. Being an intelligent creature he knows which side his bread is buttered on. He has adapted himself willingly and cheerfully to the needs of man, without ever relinquishing his natural instincts. As a house pet his habits are exemplary, and he can be trusted in any society. In spite of being pampered and adored by humans he has not lost his hunting instincts. He does not hunt for food, he hunts for pleasure, and when a hunt is started there is no let up.

My Sunbury cat, Marcus, loved to hunt what was to him big game. Living by the Thames the most easily scented out were squirrels and rats. Chasing squirrels was fun, but chasing rats was a tough assignment. He pursued a rat with the fury of a tiger and would not give up until he had made a kill. His fighting arena was always left in a bloody mess, for rats, too, are furious fighters. Marcus was lithe enough to stalk his prey and powerful enough for long jumps. He was a super cat, beautifully built — a feline athlete if ever there was one. It was heaven help the unsuspecting rodent that passed by our window or grovelled in the dust surrounding a garbage heap!

In the early days of the Fancy all cats, of the same breed, neuters or otherwise, competed against each other, but at the beginning of the century, when organised shows got on the way, schedules showed separate classes for neuters, or geldings as they were then called. The Ring Class was a special feature of the National Cat Club shows and this was a parade of all manner of cats. The owners held dainty ribbons and velvet bows as "puss" either sat or walked as the humour took him. It was observed that the main exhibits were neuters, as they were more amenable to being on leads than entire cats. This was a very spectacular class as many spectacular women were in the parade ring too.

It was not until 1939 that neuters were given important status by the Governing Council. This was done to bring together the owners of the pedigree neuters and the other championship owners. The new title to be competed for was designated with the title of premier. This was won in the same way as the honour of champion was to entire cats — three first prizes under three different judges, at three different championship shows. This innovation was a great boost for shows and very many devoted cat lovers immediately came into the Fancy. Neuters now can add to the title of premier that of grand premier, in the same was as entire cats become champions and grand champions. This means that the neuter can hold his head high all through his show career. The rules are all the same for all cats, but neuters can only compete against each other. It is tremendous fun to get involved in showing, and a new life will be opened up to you. If the exhibit is good he will win, and consider the pleasure you will get out of this unique experience. Membership of the Cat Fancy is strongly advised for the lonely at heart. The companionship of folk with the same kind of interests can be a great stimulus to a more energetic and happier life.

All people who keep cats appreciate that it is impossible to have an entire male about the house as a pet because of his objectionable habit of spraying. If he is not to be used for breeding purposes, then he must be neutered. The operation to produce this state is very simple and it is over so quickly that the cat does not know what hit him. Arrangements with the veterinary surgeon should be made in advance, and the only discipline enforced on the cat will be to go without his breakfast. This is because he will get an anaesthetic and it will be better for him if he is fasting. You will be surprised at the speed in which his appetite returns. Don't agree to a neutering operation until the cat is six months or older, and if he has not been with you at least a few weeks. It would be cruel to march him off to the veterinary surgeon before he has found his feet in his new home.

The neutering of a female is called "spaying" and is a little more exacting. It is a real operation, but it is done with such efficiency and speed today by modern veterinary surgeons, that it is not more difficult than having a tooth out. Both sexes should have sterile fillings in their sanitary trays, and the easiest and safest thing to use is just plain paper. This will not adhere to fresh skin wounds like peat moss or earth.

The freedom that a cat acquires immediately he is neutered gives him an immediate score over his breeding brothers. Freedom is the breath of life to a Siamese. They love to come and go as they please. They like to eat if they are hungry and drink if they are thirsty. They feel restricted if they are tied down to being in bed at a certain time; instead they delight in free entry or egress to their home after sundown.

A Siamese neuter above all likes to be free to keep whatever company he likes. He is no snob when it comes to fraternising with alley cats. A Siamese is never turned away if he chooses to go begging and sometimes he might do that out of sheer boredom. An acquaintance of mine once told me a story about Marcus. He used to appear at her door every morning, and she was so flattered at the attentions of a Siamese cat that she would save him something from the breakfast table, if only a piece of bacon rind. One morning he arrived with a tramp cat and together they sat patiently at the door. Two pieces of rind this time. However a morning or two later he arrived with about six homeless feline waifs. The lady thought that this was too much of a test of her hospitality, and after feeding them all she said to Marcus:

"Now see here, Sir, this is a little too much. I don't mind giving you a breakfast because you are a swank cat and I know where you come from, but I can't feed such a crowd. Remember now, you must not bring them again."

And the lady insisted that, though Marcus came regularly, he never again brought his friends.

Above: American
Grand Champion
Di Napoli's
Dresden Doll of
Dahin. Owner
Mrs Marge Naples,
California. Left:
Champion Pitapat
Sequins. Tortie
Point. Owners Mr
and Mrs Rimmer.
Photograph Anne
Cumbers.

Photograph: Hugh Smith

Champion Asuni Ki-Sun. Tortie Point.
Owners Mr and Mrs Rimmer.

Blue Point Champion Chalmi Towkay (owner Mrs Benn). Photograph: Allen Nield. And below: The first litter of Seal Point bred by the author. Photograph Dr B. R. Eustace.

Photograph: Mike Randall

Bruleon-Tu and Bruleon-Wan.
Owner Mr B. F. Burlton.

and below

Champion Spotlight Rouple.
Seal Point Male.
Owner Mrs S. Smith.

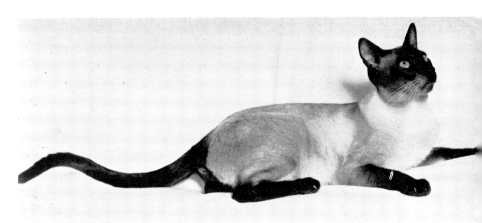

Photograph: Group 3

Champion Sislinki Topal.
Owner Mrs P. Neale.

Photograph: Hugh Smith

Champion Dunchatton Ayshah.
Owner Mrs Folkes.

Champion Kuala Caru—winner all along the line. Owner Mrs Alexander, Scotland. Photograph Mercer & Company.

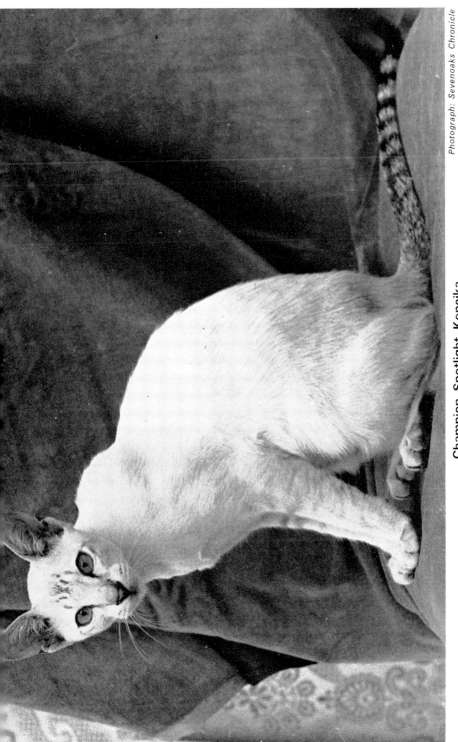

Photograph: Sevenoaks Chronicle

Champion Spotlight Kopeika
first ever Tabby Point Champion. Owned and bred by Mrs Warner.

Champion Physalis Phandah, Chocolate Point. Owner Mrs Ann Imlach. And below: Bru-Bur Honey and Tiki. Owner Mrs Burlton. Photograph Mike Randall.

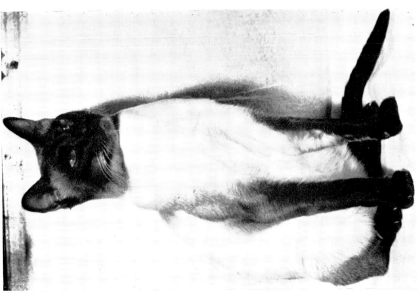

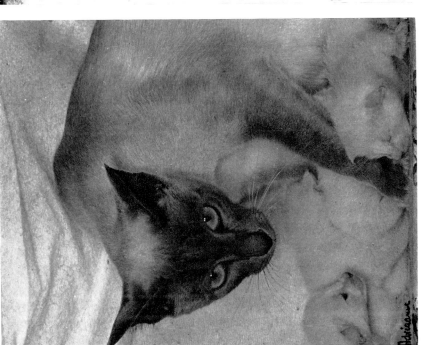

Far left: **Safari Lolita.**
Owner Mrs J. J.
Moorman, Holland.
Photograph C. A.
Adriaanse,
Amsterdam.
And left: **Champion**
Linmouth Eloika.
Seal Point. Owner
Mrs June Vogel,
Australia.

Champion Hillcross Silver Lace (Silver Tabby), and Hawthorn My Lovely (Lilac Point). Owner, the author. Photograph Dr B. R. Eustace. And below: Bru-Bur Baby. Owner Sam Scheer, U.S.A. Breeder B. F. Burlton.

Left: Taquin de St. Pierre. Chartreux male. Owner Mrs Helen Eamon, France. Photograph: Jan Claire. And above: Korat Male. Owner Mr and Mrs Ray Gardner, Arcadia. Courtesy Mrs Daphne Negus, California.

Photograph: Anne Cumbers

Exquisite Birman kitten, bred by the
late Mrs Elsie Fisher.
And below
Champion Supra Cassandra.
Owner Mrs J. Saunders.

Photograph: Fraser R. Ballantyne

Facing page: Champion Jamali Lung Chao. Brown Burmese. Owner Miss
I. M. B. O'Neill. Photograph N. E. Trowbridge.

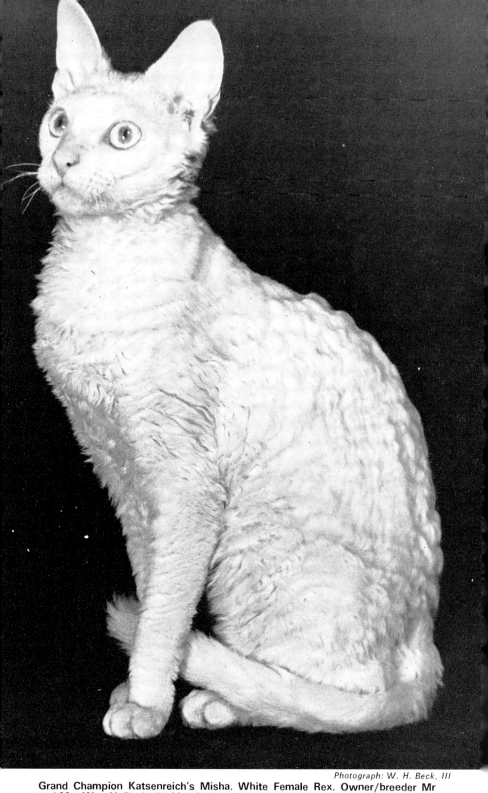

Photograph: W. H. Beck, III
Grand Champion Katsenreich's Misha. White Female Rex. Owner/breeder Mr and Mrs Wm. H. Beck, III, Maryland.

Photograph: Creszentia

Sphinx hairless. Courtesy Mrs Daphne Negus, California. And below Dooneen Dickens. Winning Tabby Point. Owner Mrs N. Macdonald, Northern Ireland.

Photograph: Anne Cumbers

Grand Champion Cymbeline Cialanga.
Owner Mrs S. Chapman. Breeder Mrs Folkes.

6. Breeding

Writers of cat books give themselves airs. They always feel that they are writing for novices, yet our real readers come from established breeders and they are kind enough to acknowledge that other people's point of view matters. Novices sometimes turn aside from the written word and so consequently will be novices all their lives. So, for the breeder who has knowledge and acknowledges that he wants more and more, the following notes are supplied.

Everyone has his own ideas about cat breeding. With the ordinary domestic cat there is no planning necessary. Black cats mate with white, red cats with creams and tabbies mate with the lot. There are no colours barred, and it appears that by instinct alone they identify each other. The end result is a happy mixture of colour, type and genes in which the over-riding feature is good health and stamina. Kittens are born with stout little hearts and an appetite for the good things in life. The traditional story of the "nine lives of a cat" fits in every detail the non-pedigreed domestic animal and her offspring. These little creatures are as hard as nails. They can overcome any obstacle and cling onto life with a rare tenacity.

The destruction of newborn kittens is a MUST if one does not want to be swamped with kittens. Good homes for even the pretty ones is not always easy to find. A breeding female can have sixteen or more kittens annually and her offspring could start reproducing at six months or younger. Where neutering is unknown the cat population can be fantastic.

If kittens have to be destroyed they should be brought to a veterinary surgeon, or sometimes to a police station, where humane methods speedily blank it into oblivion. Drowning of the young is very cruel. Supposedly drowned kittens have been known to be still alive after several hours' immersion in a bucket of water. Disposing of unwanted kittens to pet stores is not good practice among true cat lovers.

The breeding of Siamese cats is a different thing altogether. Here the emphasis is made on survival, and there are few mass exterminations. Sometimes imperfect kittens are born and these have to be painlessly destroyed. Squeamishness is no virtue in a breeder.

The question of breeding has to be gone into thoroughly and discussed with those around you. Not everyone finds the new situation a happy one. First there is the annoyance of a calling queen. This is not difficult to recognise. At first it is preceded by a restlessness and slight squeek — nothing more or less. In a matter of hours she will be on edge all over and her voice will have become so strident that she will quicken the interest of all male cats, far and near. Siamese cats can become pregnant at a very young age so vigilance is necessary.

If you are going to breed it is well to make arrangements well ahead with a stud owner and to be completely *au fait* with what is going to happen. You feel you want your little queen to mate only with a champion, and if she is a Seal Point, it is better to stick to Seal for your first venture. Mixing the colour variations will leave you in a flat spin when it comes to registration. Also, if you can at this time think straight, it would be well to select a stud whose good points would correct any faults in your breeding queen.

The queen is usually accepted for possibly three or four days, and if her condition was rightly diagnosed she will certainly be home sooner.

Cats don't mind if we gossip about them, but, on my first visit with Ming to a stud, I was flabbergasted when I rang the same day to know if all was well. Her answer was "Come immediately. Ming is insatiable. My poor boy is in a weakened condition." This was news on which I was not asked to comment. I went immediately. A stud cat has no further use for a queen whose sexual life will be completely dulled and maybe blotted out by his pressing overtures; he likes newcomers, hitherto untried.

The stud owner will know the importance of pedigree and should have already exchanged pedigrees with the queen owner. Comments from both cat owners could be useful. The stud cat cannot be held responsible for weaknesses in his progeny if the queen is not in robust health. In the interest of the stud his owner should insist on a veterinary inspection of the queen before any mating takes place. The queen may need a booster dose against F.I.E. and it is always wise to have her de-wormed just in case she has the odd worm or two. Quite a few breeders neglect this and kittens show signs of worms at a very early age. These could only have been caught from the mother. A breeding queen should be completely free of fleas. Again kittens may be infected with fleas from the mother or from the bedding that has been contaminated. Ear and eye troubles are very infectious and a barely discernible weeping eye in a mother can suddenly set up a whole litter of kittens with "poorly" eyes.

When the queen returns from the stud she should be isolated for a few days and if everything goes according to plan the first sign of pregnancy should begin to show itself at about three weeks. The nipples suddenly assume importance and are noticeably pink in colour. The queen does not call again but grows bigger every day. By about five weeks it is possible by palpation to almost count the kittens; in any event one can safely say if the litter is a large one or a small one. Too many explorations are unwise.

Soon there is great life and bustle and the little queen is fully aware of things to come. She eats ravenously and is suddenly very industrious about preparations for the birth she now anticipates. An observant breeder will notice her industry and must take pains to keep certain doors locked. It is of little use on the part of the owner to try directing the queen to this place or that. She will not be distracted; moreover she takes badly to restraint or direction by humans. Half the fun of kittening is lost if humans interfere too much.

It is always wise not to count your chickens — or in this case your kittens — before they are hatched. Sixty-five days is the normal period of gestation, and if all goes well a natural birth can be anticipated. But sometimes things go wrong and it is well to be able to recognise these signs. A period of boredom in an expectant mother, in which she appears to be listless and apathetic, disinterested in food and her surroundings, but not positively ill, may be the forerunner of something serious. Perhaps it may be the onset of a febrile illness, aggravated by pregnancy. A uterine discharge, when full-time is not more than days away, is a danger signal which no breeder can ignore. It is advisable to get in touch with your veterinary surgeon. After all, he can put your mind at rest and perhaps give her a tonic and assure you that she is alright. Things will then proceed normally.

The giving of birth is the most exciting of all events in which our cat officiates. The late Kathleen R. Williams, one of the first post war judges, breeder and author, reminiscing about her life with cats, said that after twenty years of breeding nothing could ever surpass the joy and excitement of her first litter. To her and to many others since, the arrival of a new family of Siamese was always a precious experience.

The onset of labour is nearly the same with all cats. The owner notices that something is different. Friendliness of an exaggerated nature is observed, and this may be the prelude to the great occasion. A disinclination to partake of inviting food may indicate that she has something on her mind. And she may suddenly become houseproud, unwilling to stray from her chosen haunts; she starts to line her nest with a frenzy of paper tearing. Though paper is not really an ideal litter to receive the new kittens, it is safer and cleaner during the first days; later a blanket may be introduced but it must be securely folded so that kittens cannot get buried under it.

An indication that the act of kittening has started is the appearance of a discharge, which most cats clean up immediately. The persistent licking will arouse suspicions and it is well at this time to be within call. Some cats give an agonizing cry at the moment of parturition, and this is sometimes very disconcerting especially to the squeamish. However it is not so unbearable if the kitten is pushed out immediately. The mother then is her own midwife. She bursts the transparent-like material composing the sac, and proceeds to sever the cord, thereby giving a separate existence to the new creature. She then licks the new kitten with great vigour.

Normality in everything should be the hope of every cat breeder. Lucky is the cat owner whose little queen knows how to get on with things and manages everything well, even to the severing of the cord. Of recent years many cat breeders have intimated that they must always be prepared to do this first chore in the kittening ordeal. Very undershot cats (those whose upper and lower teeth do not meet) cannot bite well; also lack of teeth may cause a willing cat to give up. Apart from these two defects some cats seem to be unable to grasp anything, either mentally or physically, and will make no attempt to sever the cord. If this becomes a human's task, use blunt sterilised scissors and cut the cord at least half an inch from the umbilicus. Watch for unnecessary bleeding.

Many Siamese breeders like to be present at the birth of kittens, saying that they can pick out winners at the moment of birth. This may be so but I could never be convinced that the pseudo-expert has all the answers. The vast majority of well-bred normal kittens take several months to establish themselves as show cats. Odd ones of outstanding length of head or body might show promise immediately, and there are the ugly ducklings which never grow into handsome swans. The long and the short of it is that it takes all sorts of kittens to make up a cat world. The plain-looking ones are usually the strongest of the litter and are ear-marked for a life of love as pet cats only.

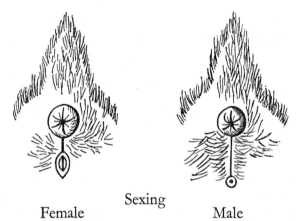

Sexing

Female   Male

Siamese kittens are born white all over. They open their eyes earlier than most other kittens. Large litters of small kittens is the usual state of affairs. Eight kittens are a common occurrence and the queen can manage beautifully.

Ming, my first Siamese, lost all her first litter through my planning machinations. Once she had set her mind on one particular abode she refused point-blank to sit it out in my specially prepared labour bed and when the kittens arrived she dragged them from place to place in a kind of frenzy or orgy. After a day of restraint, nearly all the kittens had died and the one remaining one was subjected to indescribable misery. Too late released to the freedom of the house, she continued, kitten in mouth, to seek out a place of refuge of her own planning. At the end of twenty-four hours of bustling hither and thither and being dropped brusquely when the burden became too heavy, the kitten finally gave up the ghost. If at all possible a queen should not be disturbed when she has found a fairly suitable place to give birth to her family. Perhaps after a few days she will settle down happily to rearing her family and to falling in with your housing arrangements. Young queens are the best breeders, for, sometimes when the cat is getting a bit old the novelty of kittening has worn off.

There is one event which seems to have escaped most writers about kitten management, and that is the arrival of 'Moving Day'. Nearly all cats have this on their agenda. Wherever the mother finds herself on that day, the place is just not right for her and her family. No matter how one tries to restrain her, she will get away to some new abode that seems more suitable for kitten rearing. Not all cats can count, so humans may have to help with the 'Moving Day' exit, as the little one or ones left behind might be permanently forgotten.

For the first few weeks the best kindness one can do to a new kitten is to leave it entirely to its mother. The mother will see to its needs much better than we can, especially if she herself is well fed and cleanly housed. As during her pregnancy, her appetite is enormous, so too when she has kittens around her appetite is immense. Care about the quality and quantity of the food is essential and overfeeding is a real danger, causing tummy upsets which could have serious consequences to the kittens. At about three weeks a kitten should have its first taste of solid food. Scraped raw beef is a wonderfully appetising baby food and few kittens can resist it. If one manages to eat a morsel the other kittens will follow suit. At the same time kittens should be encouraged to lap some milky food. Sometimes kittens spit and choke when they immerse their noses in milk but if they lick Farex from one's fingers they find it easier to assimilate. This gives a feeling of substance which is greatly appreciated by a young creature in search of new edible experiences. At about eight weeks kittens should be wholly independent of their mother, should be able to recognise their food trays, should be housetrained and be able to attend to their own toilet. It is a marvellous sight to see kittens of under three months old wash and tidy up like their mothers.

After a few weeks of managing for themselves, kittens should be ready to go to their new homes. They should have completed their F.I.E. vaccinations, and the veterinary surgeon would advise about worming. De-worming casually from a packet of worm powders bought in a pet store is not correct procedure when dealing with valuable stock; in fact whether they have monetary value or not, if we are responsible for their being alive we must exercise care. In the case of worming sometimes the cure is worse than the disease. Adult cats can survive drastic de-worming but not kittens. Breeding stock need special care. The perishing of embryos in the uterus is not uncommon. From my own experiences I was often in doubt, as I know a cat could clean up her pen and leave not a single trace of recent abnormal happenings. It might therefore be that an undiagnosed abortion was given the fancy name of "embryo disintegration".

Always protect your new-born kittens from prowling male cats. They can be the most ferocious predators.

At shows one soon recognises the cat that has recently overcome worm infestation. Though, being show cats, they are usually of good type, eye weakness and staring coats as well as a lack of gloss or finish point to early weakness. They are recognized as "wormy cats", though not sufficiently off colour to warrant disqualification by the veterinary surgeon. Cats cannot be cured in a day from a serious worm infestation. The building up process is long and difficult. With a history of disease in any form shows should be completely out.

It is nice to be regarded as a cat breeder of quality kittens. But reaching the top cannot come about by slipshod methods. Also two main factors have to be considered; both the sire and dam must be of strong, healthy stock if one wants to have care-free breeding days. In all one's experiences with the care and management of pedigree cats there is no situation so joyous as the raising of robust and happy kittens.

Stud work is only for the very dedicated and enthusiastic breeder. To keep the male happy he would have to be placed for public use and this entails much consideration. First he should be registered in the stud book issued by the Governing Council. He must have already proved himself. It is the duty of the stud owner to make sure that the stud's job is well done. The care of a visiting queen is a great responsibility and if it is being sent by rail the checking of timetables and syllabus can be very exacting. If at all possible the ideal thing is to have the queen delivered and collected by the owner personally.

As all breeders know, the entire male cannot be allowed the freedom of the home and a well-constructed stud house should be at his disposal. The Feline Advisory Bureau once gave their own award for what they consider good accommodation. Some cats are more prolific than others and breeding is easier when dealing with fertile queens, for return visits are not then necessary. A stud cat would require regular veterinary inspection and adequate publicity to interest the right type of cat owner, care and supervision. It is also important that stud cats have proved themselves before they are advertised for stud work. Popular breeds are more rewarding financially; it is impractical to launch out in stud work when one has a rare or uncommon breed. Location matters, for with today's high cost of travel and the difficulties and uncertainties in delivery, unless the owner can bring the queen in person many financial and other difficulties arise. As there are so many folk breeding Siamese the demand for the services of a Siamese male is always there. Even in the far north of Scotland the Siamese cat does not walk alone.

7. Kittens and Their Care

Buying a kitten is not like buying a piece of Dresden. Though both are equally valuable, the kitten cannot be put in a display cabinet and forgotten. It has to be fed and carefully tended. It has to be loved.

It is always interesting to hear from a novice or newcomer as to how he first became involved with cats. They acknowledge that radio and T.V. have been useful promoters of the cult for Siamese. There are many other things that could urge one on. Often it is prompted by a friendship with a cat lover. Maybe a visit to a house where one sees a beautiful Siamese lying sleeping in the best chair?

My first sight of a Siamese cat
There she was, elegant, beautiful, swathed in the shiniest of clinging silks, a vision of loveliness in coffee and cream — a Princess from Bangkok, an Oriental Goddess, a Queen on her throne — a Siamese cat!

(From May Eustace's *Cats in Clover*)

Yes, an arresting sight! And then there was the inanimate object — a well-polished silver cup in a prominent place on the sideboard. A "How come?" query opened up the heart of the cat owner and she told of Mitzi's delightful voyages into the very special field of show going:

Of course you know Mitzi is only her pet name. Her name for show purposes is very different. It runs to nearly twenty letters — I can't say, offhand, how many, but I do know that the registering body of the Governing Council places a limit on the number of letters they will accept for one name. I know she has the full amount. She is not a champion yet, but I have her entered for Edinburgh, and I'm sure she'll make it there.

75

These remarks aroused tremendous interest and admiration and before the sun went down on the catty scene
another admirer of felines had inscribed her name
amongst the dictionary of Siamese cat lovers.

The gist of what the novice absorbed was that:

> The breeding and exhibiting of pedigree cats is a very
> interesting and engrossing hobby, which in recent years has
> sky-rocketed to new dimensions. The pursuit is universal.
> Many of the leisured classes of the world have found outlets
> for their ambitions and fresh interest in being alive. This is a
> hobby which can be carried on so easily from one's own home,
> without any disruption to one's way of life. With more than
> fifty varieties of cat, there is a wide choice, but the Siamese cat
> is out on his own for popularity, both as a show cat and as a
> pet; also if one breeds for profit, more people want to buy
> Siamese than any other breed.

Now I address myself to the novice who is soon to
become one of the fold. After ruminating and thinking
things well over you have decided you want a Siamese
kitten! You have your husband's blessing and joy within
the family circle. A Siamese kitten it is to be. Other pets,
and more especially dogs, might be welcomed into the
picture, but they have not the exquisite appeal of a
Siamese kitten. They are bigger and clumsier about the
house and need the never-ending walks. They are noisy
too, sometimes unbearably so.

Acquiring a show cat or kitten of quality is far from
easy. Even from championship stock they do not show
up every day. Sometimes breeders are very frustrated
when the sire of a grand champion produces nothing
but a pet type kitten, and maybe from the exact same
mating as his forbears. Sometimes breeders are lucky
and can be relied upon to breed champions. But no matter
what arguments are used against the idea of an Oriental
kitten you will not be put off and are determined to try.

The first thing to do is to join a Siamese cat club of
which there are five all-variety clubs, and there are more
specialised ones: Seal Points, Blue Points, Chocolate

Points, Lilac Points, Tabby Points, Tortie Points, Cream Points — all have their own clubs. You will have to have a proposer and seconder before you are enrolled. Your friend of the "Silver Cup" can help. Addresses of secretaries change so frequently that it would be useless to name them here. Clubs hold an Annual General Meeting and new officers are sometimes approved. For accurate and prompt replies write to the secretary of the Governing Council whose address is on page 54 enclosing a stamped addressed envelope. Then try and go to shows and associate with cat folk. Usually you will find friendship and companionship in these circles; also you will see cats on exhibition, looking their best. If you are undecided about which variety you would like, a day at a show may help. You might buy at a show but do not accept delivery for a week or two; sometimes kittens pick up infection on their first outing and this might not be apparent immediately. It is generally advised not to buy on the spot, not to pay on the spot, and not to take home on the spot. And again, never buy from a pet store. Siamese kittens are not robust enough to start their independent life in stuffy, overcrowded pens, surrounded by rabbits and cavies. As a Siamese cat is a cat with a difference, so is a Siamese kitten. He is never happy to rough it.

The safest and soundest advice one can give about acquiring your first kitten is to make contact with a reliable breeder, usually introduced by a club secretary. If you want a show quality kitten you will have to pay much more than for the pet type. Don't quibble about price. Pay top price for a top kitten. You will never regret it. Think of the thrill you will feel when you present your first novice kitten at your first show. After being passed by the veterinary surgeon you will locate her pen. You will have to tidy it up a bit and then place the kitten on its new white blanket. Fill a white saucer with water, and fill your tray with moss supplied by the show organisers. Give her a last rub down with a silk scarf and whisper in her ear, "Good Luck". Intermingle with the exhibitors who have been told to "Leave the hall as judging is about to start". At 12.30 the public are admitted and the prize cards begin to appear on the pens. Imagine the excitement and the thrill you will feel when you see the first red card. You will appreciate that it is an important win as it is the open class. Quickly it is followed by other red cards and at the end of the day perhaps your kitten wins the award of best Siamese kitten. What day of thrills! How proud and happy you will be when you arrive home with your trophies! Lucky you, you bought a good kitten!

And how did you do it?

You were fortunate in that you were invited to inspect the litter before you bought. You will know enough from reading your cat books or magazines that kittens with squints or kinked tails are out. These aberrations some-times find favour with pet owners but have no place on the show bench. The very latest ruling from the Siamese Joint Advisory Board states: "That tails must be long and tapering, and not thick at the root, and must be free from kinks. A visible kink will disqualify."

The first thing you had to be sure about when you sought your kitten was to make sure that she was in good health. No matter how handsome it appeared it has little merit if it is in any sense a weakling. As soon as you have made up your mind about which sex you want and if you have decided on a female then concentrate on the females, taking note at the same time of the whole litter, observing their behaviour. A litter of ill-assorted kittens is not as satisfactory as a litter of similarly styled kittens all looking alike.

Make your selection on:

(1)   Good, strong well-nourished frame.

(2) Short, soft-lying coat. A spikey coat might mean that she was wormy.

(3) Bright blue eyes, without scaling or discharge.

(4) Clean ears. Canker, or ear mite may be troublesome in kittens.

(5) A mere sign of moisture on the nose. A running nose might mean it had a cold, and this is tiresome and difficult to treat. In a very young kitten it might mean the beginning of cat flu.

(6) Any evidence of skin disease. Ringworm is the most common and could be very serious. It is certain that all the litter would be infected, and it can be very easily passed onto humans. It would be difficult to see at a cursory glance, but reliable breeders could be trusted. Modern treatment with antibiotics is most effective. A veterinary surgeon could identify the disease with the Wood's Lamp.

(7) Any evidence of diarrhoea. This is easy to observe, and kittens should not be bought with any staining round the vent or tail.

(8) Look for fleas. They travel with such speed that it is difficult to identify them. You could infect other cats. Cat fleas are a variety all to themselves and do not attach themselves to humans.

Before leaving with your kitten make sure his papers are in order, and that he has been registered with the Governing Council, and you will get this certificate of registration as well as a transfer form, with all particulars filled in, and duly signed by the seller. Also enquire about its inoculations against Feline Infective Enteritis. Be sure also that you are given a diet sheet. Keep to the instructions given about general management. Any drastic change in diet or the pattern of its existence might set the kitten back. The first few days are the days of change and sometimes little kittens do not appreciate that a pleasant new life is about to open for them. Don't try any fancy recipes until the kitten is well established.

It is understood that your new kitten is at least three month's old. At this age it should have four meals a day. As the kitten gets older the number of meals can be reduced. Kittens are usually ravenous in the mornings. This is because they had been having, up to the time of their separation, odd snacks from mother during the night.

A simple menu, and one which I always passed on to new owners is as follows:

(1)   Breakfast. A saucer of cereal with warm milk.
(2)   Lunch. Raw minced meat (fat removed), cooked rabbit, chicken if available, and/or tinned food at about four months. Not before.
(3)   Dinner. A snack, similar to breakfast — not too much milk. Raw yolk of egg is another nourishing extra.
(4)   Supper. A little cooked fish or, if available, a repetition of dinner. Cats never get browned off with anything they find palatable — the more good things the better.

As the kitten gets older it is sensible to get her accustomed to portions of the family food. She likes cheese and biscuits, coffee and cream. This would alleviate the trouble and expense of buying tinned foods and making special catering plans. Fresh water should be always available.

And now to management.

Before your kitten arrives to take up permanent residence you will have made up your mind as to what her future habitat is to be — her sleeping quarters and arrangements for her toilet. In Denmark I have seen separate tiled cubicles adjoining the sleeping quarters. If you are starting with your first kitten, you will probably find a corner in your kitchen for her to sleep in. If there is an airing cupboard, all to the good if she can find a place where she can sleep without interfering with your clean linen or blankets. In any event there will be some place where she will find a little comfort for her first domicile. Siamese cats loathe sleeping in a basket on the floor. If given the option they would prefer to climb to go to bed. Ming, whose acquaintance you have already made, once placed her kittens in a rose bowl on the sideboard in the dining room. I don't know how they all squeezed in, but it was a case of "first come, first served" as we afterwards found that some had been left behind. This event was a sequel to "Moving Day". Ming was an intrepid explorer and found the most weird and exciting places for herself and her family. At that time our house was so large that we counted in all twenty rooms. Those were the good old days!

No matter what humans decree cats will make all major decisions for themselves; nevertheless for a new kitten there must be some guidance. It is always right to leave the sanitary tray near her sleeping quarters. There are many kinds of cat litter for use in the tray on the market today. These are very absorbent and keep odour to a minimum. Peat moss was the old reliable and this can be disposed of by absorbing it in the garden fertilizers. As the kitten gets older the tray can be put outside and very gradually the kitten will educate herself to making use of open air conveniences. Cats are cleaner than dogs for they bury their excreta, and do a real clean up after these delicate operations.

The sanitary tray should always be in reach. Cat owners should be on the alert to the placing of these trays. They should never be in sight in the bedroom, living room or cooking kitchen. No cat owners should be so enslaved with cats as to ignore the principles of ordinary hygiene. A kitten that is carefully trained in cleanliness will grow up to be a clean cat, and later if used for breeding will pass on this virtue to her progeny.

Little grooming is necessary for Siamese. A daily brush removes loose hairs. Keep an eye out for any flea infestation. Again there are many dusting powders in the pet stores which guarantee flea eradication. Be very careful with kittens especially, to brush out well after use.

Probably many cat lovers will disagree with me when I say it is not good practice for kittens to get accustomed to sleeping in bed with humans. Common sense and reasoning should see that this is not healthy for either animal or human. An occasional stretch-out on a soft eiderdown can be excused, but not as a regular resting place. When Siamese cats become adult they will nose out their own creature comforts, so it is better all round that kittens use their ingenuity too. They will always find a warm spot, and if the sun shines on any window of your house or in any corner of your garden, your Siamese will locate it.

If you are certain on the points of health, now be certain that you have found the kitten you like. Sometimes a certain little kitten will make its own little overtures to you, and you will decide that "this is it". Be absolutely sure, for there is no bringing back. Only in exceptional circumstances would the breeder be expected to take the kitten back. A returned kitten sometimes find the doors of its former home closed on it. The queen senses that something has happened and takes an instant dislike to her formerly beloved daughter. There is no such thing as buying livestock on approbation. A few days in a strange atmosphere could undo months of care.

In the days when I bred cats I found myself often in the difficult position of having to take back stock. Usually there was a good reason. In the case of death or separation in a family a cat often finds itself an outcast. This was what happened to little Nephele, the first Lilac bred in the North of England. Her type and colouring were rare, but she had one disability that precluded her from being a good breeding queen and this was that she had no bottom teeth and was unable to sever the cord after kittening. I had her neutered and she was adopted by a most saintly lady, almost in Holy Orders, living within the precincts of Durham Cathedral. The saintly lady died suddenly, and the animals found themselves abandoned and Nephele and a dog were more or less lost in the avenues and lanes surrounding the castle and university. They were observed together crouching in corners and looking wan and deserted, but if Nephele had any of the spirit of Tao — the heroine in Sheila Burnford's book — the two together might have made another *Incredible Journey*. But poor little Nephele sheltered wherever she could, meantime begging and stealing. She was abandoned too by her dog companion and standing alone she was recognised as being a Lilac Siamese by the Precenter's wife who was a good friend of mine. She instantly pinpointed her origin. It was decided that Nephele should be caught and brought back to me. Pursuit was not necessary; Nephele was so tired of wandering that she gave herself up. When I heard her story I immediately agreed to have her back.

But it was not a welcome return. Miss Ming, ageing and almost blind, abandoned her other relaxing pursuits to leave herself free to harass and attempt to do mortal injury to poor little weakened Nephele. It looked like being a war to the finish, and Ming seemed to be on the winning side. However, Brian, my eldest son, who was always a cat lover, took her home and she became a family pet.

Hawthorn Green Sleeves was another of my returning babes. Though he was much loved in his home on the river, he must have found life on the house-boat dull, especially when the family were away all day. He developed the bad habit of wool eating, which aberration is often associated with boredom. It got so bad that he consumed, almost in entirety, the complete layette being prepared for an expected baby. When the distressed owner made the complaint what could I do but to offer to take him back? After all, she did not bargain for a wool-eating cat when she came to buy a dainty pet to comfort her in her lonely hours! To place him now was not going to be easy. His new home would have to be filled more with plastics (which he abhorred) than with woollens. Perhaps I could find a home for him in the country where he would be free to wander in the ravines or gorges and find edible material which nature had produced in its own little cradle?

While I was cogitating as to where Green Sleeves' domicile might be I had a rather unexpected enquiry for a kitten from a soldier — a fully fledged lance-corporal — home from the army of occupation on the Rhine. He desperately wanted a Siamese kitten to take back to his wife. Yes, I knew he could take the kitten into Germany, but quarantine regulations would preclude him from bringing him back to England, unless he went into quarantine for six months. In England we have the most stringent restrictions of any European country. Many countries use our kennels for a certain number of months prior to shipment.

Quarantine is a word which occurs very frequently in the English vernacular. It is associated with disease and isolation. The word probably had its first meaning in Venice in 1374, when travellers suspected of having been infected with bubonic plague were isolated. In 1377 the Adriatic port of Ragusa in Yugoslavia required travellers from plague districts to remain for a month at one or two designated points before entering the city. The first quarantine station was erected in 1388 in Marseilles, where all travellers from infected ships were detained for 40 days. It is from this 40-day period of detention that the term quarantine is derived (Quaranta — forty).

The quarantine of animals was brought about by epidemics amongst dogs and cats and other animals of rabies, sometimes called hydrophobia or canine madness. It is a most dreaded and awful disease and a man bitten by a rabid dog could suffer most terrible agonies before death invariably followed. In the late years of the last century the British government was alarmed at the spread of rabies and introduced many laws to try to keep the disease in check. Quarantine establishments were set up and so strictly were the laws enforced that by 1903 the disease was almost eradicated.

But there were periods when rabies again made its appearance. This sometimes happened when dogs or cats were smuggled into England from countries where the disease was endemic. Today prosecutions and heavy fines are inflicted on people convicted of bringing in surreptitiously any cat or dog or other animal from any country, except from Ireland, the Channel Islands or the Isle of Man. Most of the enquiries for show cats come from fanciers in whose countries there are no quarantine regulations. America, Canada and South Africa are free as are most European countries. One has to be absolutely sure about the freedom to export; some countries only require a veterinary certificate as to the cat's health, but it is always right to have correct documentation.

On the whole cats do not take well to the restrictions of being in quarantine. Six months of a gaol sentence is unbearable to a human, but six months in the short life of a cat is almost a preposterous sentence. Though in the last decade things have improved enormously, and kennels are subject to strict inspection, I feel certain that there is still a feeling amongst the occupants that they are "doing time". There is an innovation. Visiting the animals is welcomed and the owners can be satisfied that all is well.

All of us at some time or other who breed cats have had occasion to learn a lot about quarantine. The sire of my Silver Tabby was imported to England after the war in an attempt to improve the breed and had to do his six months in quarantine. He had had his share of bad times and lean rations. In occupied France cats discovered that something of food value could be extracted from the bulbs in the conservatory. To this little colony of French-cum-British cats hunger was sweet sauce and they ate the bulbs and survived. But Bellever did not like being behind bars, frowned on our English rations and would eat none of our delicacies. It looked as if he might starve himself to death. Offers of steak, rabbit, chicken mince had no appeal and news was sent to his former owner in France that Bellever was on his eighth day of hunger strike. What would he eat, or what would he drink? There he was, valuable in the extreme to the Cat Fancy, prepared to die rather than help himself to the bare necessities of life laid so handsomely before him.

The little French lady knew the answers. She flew in to Heathrow and thence to the kennels.

"Comment vous portez-vous, mon chat?" she whispered, at the same time drawing from her pocket a ginger biscuit. This was as a breath of life to him for he was known in her cattery as the "Ginger Biscuit Cat". He ate his biscuit and purred quietly as he felt the gentle fingers touch his thin and weakened body. It was said that Bellever would not have survived without the sound of his native tongue in his ear and the taste of his beloved ginger biscuit in his mouth. Cats are sometimes queer creatures.

All cats can be destructive on soft furnishings but, sad to say, Siamese can be more destructive than most. Training starts with kittens. Never ignore a kitten when he starts clawing at furniture. Immediately warn him off by tipping him with a newspaper and showing displeasure. If he thinks he can get away with it then he will persist, but he is intelligent enough to understand your wishes, and can be trained. Scratching boards are sold in most pet stores and are very useful indeed. If not available then make one yourself. Cover an old chair with a carpet or a piece of old linen. It must be something into which he can stick his claws. Try to arrange to have the decoy smelling of catmint. If he is barred from the living room where all the good furnishings are, then he will settle for the old chair and, in time, get attached to it. Tree trunks are used by most cats as scratching posts, and one is lucky to have one near the cats' exit door.

Many fastidious cat owners, especially in the States, have their cats declawed. This operation is called onychectomy, and has to be performed by a veterinary surgeon. In Britain the practice is frowned on, and no cat which has been declawed will be accepted at a show.

Sometimes one is queried about a cat's reactions to uncommon events in the home. The arrival of a new baby cannot be ignored and care should be taken to ensure that the baby is never in a position where the cat might lie near or on its face, or in some way endanger its life. I was very nervous when I heard that Marcus' owner was expecting her first baby. I warned Una to take care, but she afterwards told me that the only reaction that came from Marcus was to ask to leave the room every time the baby appeared. He persevered with his feline snub until the baby became a real person, sitting up and taking notice.

About health, do not set yourself up as an expert. Unqualified help may be very harmful. It is sometimes rather nauseating and pathetic to hear fanciers hand out glib diagnoses without having seen the invalid. In spite of all that is written and spoken in the veterinary field we still have the dangerous "know-alls", who can cure all ills. DO NOT be a home doctor unless you have special gifts for healing.

Nevertheless it is beneficial to be able to take temperatures and assess signs of serious illness, but, realize your own limitations, and consult a veterinary surgeon without delay. If you feel the case is urgent and if, in the first instance, you speak on the telephone, listen carefully to the instructions. If these are understood and applied correctly you may be able to alleviate suffering.

To be the owner of a beautiful, well-bred Siamese kitten is something to be proud of. To be able to look after it and see it grow in health and strength is a very great thrill indeed. There are few such rewarding situations in life, especially to a cat lover.

But the Siamese kitten must not be to you only a "he", "she", or "it". The naming of it must not be overlooked. You will see to it that it has been registered with the Governing Council concerned with your cat affairs. This will depend on where you live. It is most probable that the official name will not please you, for it may be clumsy or too high-sounding. You will think out a pet name, and one that will be easy to pronounce. Please do not settle for such ordinary names as Pansy, Daisy or Dolly. From the very beginning you must treat the newcomer with dignity and pride.

In kennels names play an even more important part; a lonely, listless cat can sometimes come to life at the sound of its name.

I once had a cat for a lengthy stay. Again though I knew her registered name, and had all particulars tabulated, I failed to ascertain her pet name. However, on the spur of the moment, we just called her Abigail, after her owner. The name seemed to fit the cat as well as it did the demure little lady. Imagine my dismay when she called to collect her cat, and my small grandson called vociferously, "A-B-I-G-A-I-L", and swish! From under the gooseberry bush the cat emerged immediately. There was such a joyous re-union that my misdemeanour was overlooked. I was most embarrassed but no explanations were necessary. The two Abigails went away full of the joys of life.

8. Goodbye to all that

I, and Pangur Ban, my cat,
'Tis a like task we are at;
Hunting mice is his delight,
Hunting Words I sit all night.
                    Old Irish Translation

Everyone loves to reminisce. This is a spiritual exercise which is good for the mind and the body. To reminisce about old times and old friends is pleasant indeed, but to include cats in the message is something quite special to the heart of a cat lover.

My dedication to cats has occupied almost my whole life. In my young days there was just the succession of the homely fireside cats who came and went as they pleased but who always knew where to return for food and comfort:

> Dynasties of cats, as numerous as those of the Egyptian kings succeeded each other in my dwelling. One after another they were swept away by accident, by flight, by death. All were loved and regretted; but life is made up of oblivion, and the memory of cats dies out like the memory of men.
> Theophile Gautier

To create my Siamese dynasty I am thinking back to about 1950. It was about that time when I commenced to breed Siamese kittens, and first associate with people in the cat world. During that period, the first years were spent as a breeder and exhibitor, and the second half as a judge. As a judge I have been lucky to have been able to get around and associate with some of the finest people in the world. In Britain judges do not receive fees as they do in the States, but they do not come away empty-handed; today I have around me many souvenirs and trinkets given by show managers as mementos of each show at which I officiated.

Reminiscing on past scenes I find there was good reasoning in what the French poet wrote in the eighteenth century:

> Refined and delicate natures understand the cat. Women, poets, and artists hold it in great esteem, for they recognise the exquisite delicacy of its nervous system; indeed, only coarse natures fail to discern the natural distinction of the cat.
>
> Champfleury, *Les Chats*, 1885

So, for me "coarse natures" were out.

I went into the company of the élite. The Siamese Cat Association first nominated me as a judge, and I was inducted into the new life by Mrs. Elizabeth Towe and Mrs. Lucy Price. First I had to complete my stewarding engagements, which in all were more than twenty. My first exciting stewarding engagement was with the late Miss Kathleen Yorke, who was at that time the Chairman of the Governing Council. She gave me great counsel and splendid advice; in fact I was so happy on that first day that I felt I was almost a judge. She warned me about the careful handling of cats, and just as I was returning a champion to his pen he turned round and gave me a good, hard bite. Fortunately no one noticed me. I licked the wound and kept quiet about it, but I decided that after all stewarding was not all that fun. If I had gone home streaming with blood I knew my husband would never have agreed to another such engagement, and though I continued stewarding for another twenty or so shows that was the last hard bite I ever got. I took good care of that. I didn't mind what a judge thought about me, if I saw a fight coming I ducked.

Having satisfied the Council as to my character and my ability I was appointed, not with too much harmony, as a probationer judge, and my first exemption show was unforgettable. It took place at Bingley, Yorkshire. The day before the show the show manager rang me to say, "It has been raining here for days and the ground has turned into a quagmire. Be sure to wear Wellingtons." I took her advice though I loathed them and never kept them. I rushed out and bought myself a pair. It was still raining when I checked in at the hotel on the Friday night. I congratulated myself on being wisely equipped for any cloud burst.

"Morning tea at eight with the paper?" queried the night porter.

"Yes," I said, pleased with the excellent service offered. However, there arose a dilemma. When it came to undressing, try though I might I could not get the boots off. I did everything I could. I lay on the floor. I sat on the bed. I clung to the window ledge, and I pulled and I pulled. To no avail. I had to go to bed in my boots. Imagine my shame when I opened the door in the morning to admit the night porter, and there was I standing in my short nightie and still in my boots! Oh, my poor feet! Never will I forget how they felt after a hard day's judging and a train journey home which took me long into the night.

Another exemption show that will always make me laugh was one in which our president, Mrs. E. Towe, was guest of honour. The Mayor was coming to York to honour the cats and the president. And lo and behold! before the grand opening occurred there was our president off out at the entrance on the arm of the chauffeur — a case of mistaken identity! Right enough — when we saw the Mayor afterwards we decided that she had made a better choice!

We have had many amusing episodes on British railways. Coming back on the sleeper from Glasgow, we came to a stop where we thought we had arrived at King's Cross. Laughs were heard coming from Elizabeth's sleeper. We were stationary at a siding where cows were looking in the window. A sense of humour was always a MUST when travelling.

A few weeks later I had an assignation to judge Seal Point males at Chester. On the journey I thought of myself as being very lucky to be doing Seals, for at that time I knew there were so many good ones about that my task was not going to be easy. There is nothing a judge likes better than good competition. It is very off-putting when you take your first look and you see a row of little round heads and googly eyes, staring out at you lovingly from their pens. These are the pet cats that one just wants to cuddle, and not to judge, and these kinds of cats follow a pattern. If you read the catalogue properly and perhaps ask to see a pedigree form, you will observe certain close relatives — in fact this show is mostly of cousins. Usually they inherit the bad points from this or that sire, and no points worth noticing from this or that dam.

I got to Chester nice and early. "Sorry," said the hotel receptionist, "you are not booked in here."

"Oh, yes, I am," I replied truculently, "and here is the letter from the show manager."

"Yes," said the receptionist, "but you are a week too early."

And so I was. Meekly I asked about trains back to Euston. None now till morning.

"Dinner is now being served, and we have rooms to spare," said the nice receptionist.

Dejectedly I sallied forth. Lovely hotel. Lovely views. Lovely people, but now at my own expense.

Amongst the "lovely people" was a very nice man who

seemed to be at a very loose end. He heard of my dilemma and offered to take me out to show me some of the sights of the beautiful city of Chester.

"Yes, thank you, in the morning perhaps," I answered most cordially, but before the sun rose I was up. I grabbed my breakfast, the entire menu which I would eat or die. I rushed to the station in time to catch the boat train, and that was all. I never looked up and never saw the sights. It just goes to show that judges have to always be on their mettle.

It is nice to cast a nostalgic eye back on the very many pleasant comings and goings — show-wise — that I undertook with the other judges through the years. One thing was certain. Our doings sometimes excited curiosity and once on a train the other occupiers of the carriage were most intrigued to identify this strange assembly of women accompanied by one charming and good-looking man. They speculated, was he being kidnapped? Then they heard such names as Sianjo Lin-Sarah — Kirsta Stephano — Kaloke Giselle — and they were more intrigued then ever. Were we travellers from outer space or just patients on parole from a loony bin? Certainly our bearing and demeanour were different from the ordinary, we were worth being observed. There was still astonishment on many faces when the train stopped and the journey ended.

And then there was the television star of the Blue Peter programme, Jason. This beautiful cat projected the Siamese image into many homes in Britain. His gentleness and quiet reserve won universal appeal. Visiting dog celebrities or strange cats on the programme made no impression on him. He was calm and beautiful and did the job he was paid for. Under the protecting arms of his caretaker-owner, Mrs E. Menezes, he accompanied the judges on many long and arduous journeys. As a draw he was Number One cat. Many champions and grand

champions were on show but the cry from the young
fanciers was always, "Where is Jason?" On exhibition
at Olympia the crowds had to be controlled by officers
of the law.

But now, alas! he has passed on to the Happy Hunting
Ground where, we hope, his spirit will find eternal peace
with the many gentle and loving cats that have gone
before him.

When one is judging one meets very exciting and
interesting people. I was privileged to be the guest of Mrs.
Vivian Marx-Nielson, Denmark's most honoured cat
fancier. In her mansion in Odense I saw how royal cats
should live.

Not all our Siamese owners have royal connections;
nevertheless they are associated with royal cats. As a
judge and a writer my ears are more receptive than most
when it comes to Siamese lore. During a show many
exhibitors, stimulated by love and devotion for their cats,
have poured poetry and romance into my ears. Especially
is this noticeable when an exhibit is wearing his newly-
won honours for the first time. The delight and eagerness
to talk suddenly illuminates the face of the cat owner. She
is so proud that she cannot be restrained. She must talk
especially if I have given him his first challenge certificate.
She feels that merely by looking at him I have no idea of
his real self.

"We are so pleased that you like Pip. Don't you think
his coat is exquisite? Also his points are really RED. My
husband and I attribute this to his liking for beetroot,"
said one.

"Well, I never," I replied, thinking inwardly there's
nothing as odd as folks.

Then another felt an incubus to talk about his cat's
sex life.

"Though we have many requests from queen owners
to use him for stud, he simply has no interest in females.

Do you think he should have some hormone treatment?"
Yes and No. Methought these were very personal matters
for open discussion.

"And did you like his real name — Zeus?" said a
long-haired, bearded relation. "We called him after the
king of Olympian Gods."

Looking at the face before me, I felt it was king-like
too. Using a colloquialism, I feel it is not really 'cricket'
to report on tales told from the exuberant heart of a
winning exhibit; for published anecdotes I prefer to make
my own cats the scapegoats, and a study of Ming, my
first Siamese, will satisfy my need to tell tales. Because
she came into our lives following a succession of simple,
loving and entirely guileless cats, her performance
enraptured us all. All through her long life she was a
compulsive thief, and now, reminiscing, I would say her
thefts of food were largely our own fault. We were
absolutely naive in our feeding methods. Though not
exactly a wartime cat, brought up like humans on short-
ages, her pedigree showed that her grandsire was
Killed By Enemy Action. Certainly in the late forties
rationing was still with us.

Ming's breeder, living in a mansion which must
always have been full and plenty, hinted that Ming was
a fish lover and a useful meal easily procured from a fish
shop, was a cod's head; also now at last kippers were in
the shops which she adored. She was adult when I bought
her, and she was such a fat little cat that no one would
believe she had reached maturity on bones and scraps.
However, to her, kippers were always a delicious sweet-
meat.

We did not know Ming very well when we surprised
her purloining a kipper from the larder. Opening the
door suddenly Ming came out on all fours trailing on the
floor in a *mea culpa* attitude. Even if we did not know
what she was up to her contrite crawl condemned her.

All through her thieving life she confessed on humble knees. Sometimes we made little of Ming's thieving, but there was one occasion when I was, most certainly, not amused. Once when going to the kitchen to collect a nicely laid tray which had been got ready for my special friend, Dolly, Ming hurried past me, licking her lips. "Eh! what now?" I thought. She had been helping herself to the cream for the morning coffee. She had a nose that could smell out anything. She was born a thief and nothing could alter this.

When Ming was boarded out with a friend — this was before her first official entry to dreaded kennels — she sat obstinately in a corner in the friendly house and refused to eat. This was her way of making a protest. Maud, who was her hostess, and well knew of Ming's dishonest practices, became desperate when three or four days of starvation looked like continuing. She thought up a ruse. If Ming could feel that she was stealing, she would steal to survive. Maud put a sausage on the pan in the kitchen, and left, making sure that Ming heard her go. She peeped through the outside kitchen window, and silently surveyed the scene. The gas had been turned off but a smell of cooking pervaded the kitchen. She saw Ming showing interest, and then carefully dismount from the table and approach very stealthily in the direction from which the odour came. Very carefully, for she knew what a burn felt like, she purloined the sausage. She had a little bite and licked her lips. Then she went back for more, and in a day or two her appetite returned to normal. Dishonesty had saved her life.

Without any show points whatever she won all hearts with her winsomeness and charm. Though she was never restricted to being enclosed in runs like other show cats I owned, she often squeezed herself in with stud cats or handsome kittens, just for their company. But not always. Sometimes she was an aloof little cat who sat by herself

in the bed of catmint, breathing in the perfume which
was reminiscent of happier days, and other times she
nestled under a privet hedge and counted the sunbeams
and the earthworms in a dream world of her own.

There were just the odd occasions when Ming got
mixed up with the common fry and on one occasion a
very special somebody from our newly resuscitated
Northern cat club came to buy a kitten. As she came
accompanied by a car full of followers I did not relish
bringing the whole party indoors so I told them to go
and look at the cats in the outside common cattery, and
I would join them presently. As they did not really know
what they wanted their swapping and changing appalled
me. At that particular time I was fortunate in having a
nice litter of Blue Points, and they were playing with the
Seals. They put on a great show, running up and down
the trees and exuding good spirits. Aside, and quietly
contemplative, sat little Ming. Then it was suddenly
decided and it was Grandma who spoke: "We will have
that little fellow over there with the black face," pointing
at Ming.

Poor little cat! What a thing to say about a handsome
cat! Naturally I refused, saying that Ming was not for
sale. Very reluctantly they took away a nice little Blue
Point male which was far too good to be ignored from
the show point of view. Later I persuaded them to show
the kitten, and he won well as a neuter. Still, they never
really cottoned onto Blue Points, and years later when I
asked about Chang the reply was: "Chang is alright, but
I was always sorry that I didn't have the little fellow with
the black face."

Later in life I had another unusual neuter called
Marcus, my Sunbury cat. He came home one day carrying
a ball of newly wound wool. He didn't attempt to play
with it but left it on the hearth and forgot about it. And
so should I had he not arrived a day or two later with

a similar ball, again fresh from the knitter's house. And again came a third ball. I appreciated that the disappearance of knitting wool could be such an embarrassment so I put the three balls side by side in the front window. Soon a neighbour identified them, saying, "Thank goodness for my sanity. I was so certain that I wound the wool and put it in a certain place, and as there was nobody else in the house I could not believe my eyes when I found them missing. The first one was not so bad but when it came to a second and a third disappearing so mysteriously I felt I was really going crackers."

It seemed that Marcus was able to get through the window of the neighbour's cottage, and make quite a lot of fun for himself. In addition to taking away balls of wool he had been regularly tearing the daily newspaper to shreds before it had been read, and making his getaway without being noticed. Not that he was ever furtive in his movements, he did not know what stealing meant. He was a proud cat.

There is a certain bond between cat lovers which could almost be called an *entente cordiale*. Though the great Irish Sea divides us I still feel drawn to the folks who made room for me in their little circle. This friendship could never be broken. Somewhere in at the start was a little Siamese cat.

Mrs. Anne Aslin, the owner and breeder of the first Siamese grand champion in Britain, received my congratulations by complimenting me on putting her on the right track when showing cats. I had no memory of it and was deeply grateful to her for her kind remarks, which were:

> At a Siamese show held in Hove in 1964, I showed a cat under you which you had passed over. When I asked you for your comments you said that the exhibit was not really a show cat. Its eyes were too round and it was an inch too short in the head. There was not enough width between the ears. Needless to say, I went home without a card, and will always remember

and thank you for giving me my first lesson. After that I knew what to look for, and left my pet cats at home.

And Anne has gone on and on breeding and showing only the best. I keep track of my friend's good fortune in the pages of *Fur and Feather*, which is now my bible, as precious a reading for me as are the Gospels.

I met Mr. and Mrs. C. Dessauer at one of their early shows and we came round to talking of their first Siamese. To a cat lover this first Siamese is the most important cat in the universe, and all breeders have a tale to tell of this new creature in their midst. Mr. Dessauer's extract from *Mayfield's Story* is quoted below. Incidentally *Mayfields* was the prefix the Dessauer's adopted for their Siamese dynasty:

> We wanted a pet for our thirteen year old son. A puppy was the popular choice, but I could not see myself dragging a reluctant puppy for his nightly stroll in the wind and rain, so when a kitten was suggested Anthony acquiesced. We had seen our first Siamese in Switzerland and were enraptured with it. At that time it was very difficult to get a kitten, so, after much searching we got Sheeba — the dearest little creature we had ever set eyes on. When it came to us it was very nervous and disliked doorbells. When the doorbell rang — away! Sheeba would be missing for maybe half a day, sometimes squeezed in at the back of the bath. And now seven years later she still dislikes doorbells and strangers. And with her strange little quirks, we love her and to us there will never be another Sheeba.

Sir Compton Mackenzie, so many years the president of the Siamese Cat Club, loved to demonstrate his extraordinary devotion to cats and to Siamese in particular. He never missed the opportunity to demonstrate to dog lovers on whose side he was on. Up to the time of his death Siamese cats were *persona grata* with the great intellectual. We always felt there was a wide barrier between cat lovers and dog lovers, yet, many of our most enthusiastic fanciers have come to us via the dog.

Dog worship in this country is largely a twentieth century

product, and may be attributed to the gradual destruction of the individual. Man now requires a dog to confirm his belief in the existence of a superior animal called Homo Sapiens. Men like dogs because they provide them with the esteem which Victorian man demanded from women: women like dogs because they are less exacting and more faithful than men.

People sometimes say to me that they are fond of Siamese cats because they are so much like dogs. I always reply that I am fond of Chows and Pekinese because they possess some of the dignity and independence of cats.

Sir Compton Mackenzie

Mrs. Oona Henderson was a dog breeder. She sent me the following notes about her Montem cats:

I myself used to be a devoted dog breeder but developed a great hankering for a Siamese but just did not dare take the plunge, until one summer evening eleven years ago when some friends, who knew of my feelings, drove up unexpectedly and presented me with a Chocolate-pointed kitten and I was completely absorbed and my life wholly changed! Since then cats have taken over my life and the total at present is 15 cats to only five dogs. I now keep just Siamese of most colours, and Silver Tabbies, marbled and spotted. My prefix is Montem. Cats are my greatest interest in life now, and I find them a great comfort and joy to me, and could not bear to live without them.

Most fanciers like to read about cats. It is certain too that dedicated fanciers are very interested in happenings of their neighbours. For specific news they must read cat books and periodicals. The official organ of the Governing Council is the little fortnightly publication, printed in its own works at Idle, Bradford, Yorkshire — *Fur and Feather*. This started life in a humble way, costing the noble sum of one penny. That was in 1919, when the tenor of all our lives was on a different keel from what it is today. At the present time the reading of *Fur and Feather* is a MUST to the show goer. In addition to advertisements of cats and kittens for sale and stud notices, it contained news from the clubs, letters from the happy and not-so-happy. The editor publishes all matter appertaining to the well-being of the cat, and the up-grading or down-grading of the individuals. The judge's show reports are written up after every show and for this alone subscribers think they get their money's worth. Now, however, space is very limited and judges only report on open class winners; club classes, of which there are very many, have to be omitted. For very eager exhibitors most show managers will sell a marked catalogue, which gives all the winning cats, and for those who don't know, the name and number of the cat is followed by its age, name of sire and dam, name of owner and breeder, and addresses can be found at the end of the catalogue.

At one time *Fur and Feather* published weekly the names and particulars of all registered kittens. To see the name of one's first litter printed in an important cat magazine was one of the greatest thrills a new breeder could experience.

Mrs. Ashford, a sub-editor, scans the show scene and writes up all the interesting news. She also keeps well in touch with the Governing Council and explains any new pronouncements to her readers. She is very interested in the well-being of cats, and attends all veterinary seminars, making the findings known to her readers.

Several magazines and cat periodicals have disappeared during the last decade. *Our Cats*, published by the late Arthur Cowlishaw, could not find a successor to carry on when he died. This was a delightful little extra to *Fur and Feather*, and it was a pity to see it fade out. *Cats and Kittens*, published by Mr. and Mrs. France, again could not survive. Several interested cat lovers, with journalistic experience, have tried to establish new papers or magazines that would deal with cats only, but have been unsuccessful. *Fur and Feather* embraces nearly all fur and feathery creatures, otherwise it, too, might have to set a different scene.

Another excellent way fanciers have found to help to keep in touch with each other has been the issues of club newsletters. These are very informative, especially to Siamese breeders. The Foreign White Society, when it was carefully treated with good editorship and careful research, produced a most informative and delightful newsletter. This breed was developed on highly scientific lines, and has been a great victory for those who were in at the beginning.

Since the war the passing years have taken from us some of our most vital and interesting Siamese judges. Those I have known and worked with were Miss Kathleen Yorke, Miss Kit Wilson, Mrs. K. R. Williams, Mr. Brian Stirling-Webb, Mrs. Elsie Kent, Mrs. Merry, Mrs. Denham, Mrs. Lamb, Mrs. G. Hindley and Mrs. Ferguson.

A new generation of judges is gradually taking over. For the promotion of Siamese judges there is a Joint Advisory Committee. This consists of elected representatives of the Siamese clubs. They receive applications from prospective judges, and, if considered worthy, they are passed by a panel of senior judges and their names forwarded to the Governing Council for approval. They are then appointed as probationer judges, and if they are proved worthy, they move up to full judges within a year or two. The opportunity to be a judge is open to all fanciers who satisfy the regulations about stewarding engagements, breeding, showing, with the date on which they registered their prefix being the most important. Several matters influence the decision of the selectors, and some aspirants never make the grade, which is difficult to understand. Membership of the Cat Fancy is open to all. The owner of a neutered pedigree cat has as much right to be there as the important breeder of pedigree cats.

In Ireland we have a very healthy Cat Fancy, run on

excellent lines, and patterned exactly on the British Council. Most of the officiating judges come from England, and judging is similar in results to that of England. The same standard of points is applied, yet the English Council does not recognise our champions as true blues. Most, if not all, of the foundation stock are English imports. Championship shows are run annually in Dublin, Dun Laoghaire, and Cork and many small exemption shows are organised in varying venues throughout Ireland. While this island is so divided it is a great joy to see so many of our exhibitors come from over the border. In the Cat Fancy at least, they are all of one mind and one soul.

The most popular cat is, as elsewhere, the Siamese.

And now I am nearing the end of my trail. The week-end trek across Britain is over. The show scene has folded up. My last Christmas greetings are worth recording. When I got off the train at Newcastle-upon-Tyne I was suddenly alerted to the fact that Christmas was upon us. I rushed to the nearest newsagent to get my last minute cards. A first glance revealed only horrors — holly berries and jingle bells! I was about to leave when, to my great relief, I saw a box of beautiful views of the old Tyne Bridge, copied from a well-known etching. These were great. How nice to send to Geordie exiles of which I knew so many! or, how nice for anyone! how really nice! They were expensive but they were classy. I didn't read the wish. Who cares, when the pictures are so nice? But one of the recipients did care and I got this curt reply from a friend in Copenhagen:

> Thanks dear, it was nice of you to remember me, but, "Happy birthday" to whom? It was not my husband's or mine, or my cat's.

So that was one greeting card that misfired. The response mostly brought laughs, for whatever the greetings spelled out, it was generally agreed that it was just a friendly greeting from one cat lover to another.

*TO A SIAMESE CAT**
(June 1930-December 1942)

I shall walk in the sun alone
Whose golden light you loved:
I shall sleep alone
And, stirring, touch an empty place:
I shall write uninterrupted
(Would that your gentle paw
Could stay my moving pen just once again!).

I shall see beauty
But none to match your living grace:
I shall hear music
But not so sweet as the droning song
With which you loved me.

I shall fill my days
But I shall not, cannot forget:
Sleep soft, dear friend,
For while I live you shall not die.

Michael Joseph

*With acknowledgement to Mrs. Michael Joseph.